High Fashion

High Fashion

THE 20TH
CENTURY
DECADE
BY DECADE

Thames & Hudson

WITH 166 ILLUSTRATIONS

First published in the United Kingdom in 2016 by
Thames & Hudson Ltd, 181A High Holborn, London WC1V 7QX

© 2015 Quid Publishing
Book design by Tony Seddon
Cover illustration: Anna Ismagilova

British Library Cataloguing-in-Publication Data
A catalogue record for this book is available from the British Library

ISBN 978-0-500-51807-6

Printed and bound in China by 1010 Printing Group Ltd.

To find out about all our publications, please visit **www.thamesandhudson.com**.
There you can subscribe to our e-newsletter, browse or download our current
catalogue, and buy any titles that are in print.

Contents

Introduction

We have an intimate, corporeal relationship with clothing. It accompanies us every day of our lives; its form and function are fulfilled by our own bodies. As such, we interact with it in a completely different way than we do with most other products of design.

This personal relationship means that clothes have a particularly expressive function: they allow us to construct a visual identity that is both individual and social at the same time. Our clothes say something about us as individuals, but also about the 'tribe' we belong to. Furthermore, they function as a wider visual language that can tell us a lot about the time, place and society in which they were created and worn.

This interactive use and relationship between us and our clothes means that we all have some understanding of them – however, the second we replace the word 'clothes' with 'fashion', that understanding begins to vary wildly from person to person.

Because fashion is defined in such varied ways by individuals, the press and academics, it seems important to explain from the outset how the term is going be used in this book, to avoid any risk of vagueness or confusion.

I've used the word 'clothing' so far, but of course not all clothes are fashion. While anthropologists agree that, throughout history, people have decorated their bodies in one way or another for social reasons, fashion is not merely about cloaking or adorning the body. If it were that simple, we couldn't talk about things being 'in' or 'out' of fashion, nor define something as 'so last season'. These journalistic stock phrases can help us begin to understand what makes clothing different from fashion: fashion is dress that continually changes and renews its own expressive format.

Fashion historians generally agree that it is during the fifteenth century that a cyclical change in adornment becomes noticeable enough to allow us to start speaking of 'fashion'. From that point onwards, the French and Italian elite (court society) adopted new styles and colours that changed the course of fashionable dressing. The time frames of these cycles that saw certain styles going in and out of use were remarkably long compared to today's turnover of what is 'in fashion'. This is down to many factors but, aside from production limitations, the most important one is that until we get to the middle of the nineteenth century we have no clearly defined or organised fashion business model.

This business model was introduced around 1858 by the father of Haute Couture, the English fashion designer Charles Frederick Worth. When he founded the Haute Couture system in nineteenth-century Paris, Worth showed himself to be both a visionary designer and a canny businessman. The changes he introduced to the rather haphazard business of dressmaking laid the foundations for today's international fashion industry and helped refine our modern definition of the term 'fashion'.

House of Worth

Though he was originally from provincial Lincolnshire, Charles Worth realised that Paris had been the capital of luxury and good taste since the reign of Louis XIV, and thus he decamped there to found his business. 'Haute Couture' translates from the French as 'elevated sewing' or 'high-quality sewing/work', and this was exactly what Maison Worth offered its clients: luxurious, innovative and exquisite garments.

This was not, however, what set his business apart from the many dressmakers before him; one need only visit a historic dress collection, or look through a lavishly illustrated fashion history tome, to see just how exquisite, original and often decadent the fashions of the elite had been throughout the previous centuries. What made Worth's approach unique was not a radical change in design, but the fact that he introduced the idea of the 'collection'. By presenting a group of new, finished garments twice a year, he effectively imposed a timetable

Opposite People have a corporeal relationship with clothes and interact more intimately with garments than any other form of design. Clothes have both a physical and a psychological function that goes far beyond mere protection for warmth, modesty or comfort.

Above *Charles Frederick Worth, aged 30. The son of an English solicitor, he moved to Paris when he was 21 years old, without money, connections or command of the French language. From such unlikely beginnings he went on to found the House of Worth and became the father of Haute Couture.*

Above *The House of Worth at 7, Rue de la Paix, Paris, where Charles Worth established his fashion house that drew in a wealthy and famous clientele, from royalty to stage stars.*

Opposite *An exquisite gala dress, constructed with layers of white tulle and glittering with gold leaf, dominates a portrait of one of Worth's wealthy clientele: the Empress Elisabeth of Austria, painted by Franz Winterhalter in 1865. The royal stamp of approval was the nineteenth-century equivalent of modern celebrity endorsement.*

on creativity, artistic innovation and consumption – because with the introduction of each new collection, by extension, he of course made everything that went before 'old-fashioned', thereby defining a limited lifespan for fashionable garments.

Worth's success was immediate and soon many others followed in his footsteps, imitating his business model. In 1868, La Chambre Syndicale de la Haute Couture was founded by Worth and his sons in an attempt to organise and regulate this growing group of 'elite' designers and their maisons (fashion houses), and to try to prevent the copying of their designs.

Haute Couture became synonymous with good taste, novelty and luxury, and cemented Paris's identity as the epicentre of fashion. Clients travelled from across the globe to purchase their original Haute Couture gowns in the splendour and privacy of the sumptuous Parisian salons. Here they were treated to private fashion parades to aid them in their purchasing choices, and as all garments were custom-made – each one was entirely original – clients were required to come in for several fittings to make sure everything was just right. This service naturally came with an exorbitant price tag, but the cachet of an original, one-off Worth, combined with the exquisite fit and construction of the gowns, affirmed the elite status of the wearer, which in a class-obsessed society was considered to be worth every penny.

Prerogative of the Few, Distraction of the Many

So we see that, alongside continual change, originality and elitism are also hallmarks of fashion. In the nineteenth century, the elite (not only the aristocracy, but now also the new economic elite that had emerged from the Industrial Revolution) was the only group in society able to engage with fashion. Consequently, high status, a known designer name, expense and originality became intrinsically linked. Those in the upper echelons of society were seen to set the tone of fashion, and to be the arbiters of good taste.

The elite had always used clothes to signal their difference in status from others, which is why originality and uniqueness were such important concepts to them. Worth understood this desire for distinction and offered each client a one-off design. The uniqueness often resided in the way the dress was decorated and trimmed, with only minor adjustments to the actual silhouette from one dress to the next. Originality was thus something linked to both innovation of design and the finished product.

The importance of originality and the protection of original fashion design was already being discussed in the latter decades of the nineteenth century – hence the Chambre Syndicale's attempts at protecting designers' work. However, the discussion really gained in importance throughout the twentieth century, when the development of mass production and a mass market for fashion posed an increasing threat.

The first five decades of the twentieth century see a clear line between what Haute Couture fashions proposed and what was being worn by 'ordinary' women. However, there was a trickling down of styles from the upper to the lower echelons. This not only provides evidence of the continued dominance of Haute Couture designers and their clients as tastemakers, but also highlights the inherently aspirational element of fashion. The elite adopts a new fashion, which triggers the group directly below them to try and adopt it; the one directly below these does the same, and so on. The result is twofold. Firstly, the fashion becomes increasingly diluted, design-wise, on its way down the social ladder, due to financial and practical constraints, until at the lowest level the garments only vaguely resemble the original concept. Secondly, at the same time this system of emulation propels fashion forward, since the elite, who used the original fashion to affirm their status and engagement with novelty, must now search for something even newer, to redress the balance and ensure that social distinctions do not become blurred. This social need for change in fashion was exactly what Worth translated into his business model through his introduction of collections.

While in the mid-nineteenth century there was no such thing as ready-to-wear fashion, nowadays clothing inspired by high-end fashion is available to all on the high street. This highlights the fact that part of the definition of fashion involves acknowledging the originator of the design. What is available at budget high-street stores may resemble the styles seen on catwalks, but these garments are merely inspired by the catwalk, and thus devoid of originality or design innovation. They are fashionable but they are not fashion.

Forces of Change

Despite this evidence that the trickle-down effect is still at work, it does not follow that this influence has remained unchanged since 1858. At several points during the twentieth century, significant challenges to the fashion status quo have cropped up, and certain changes or realignments have been introduced.

For many fashion historians, the most radical changes came after World War Two, a period that saw emerging designers look for inspiration towards young, non-elitist groups – people who had previously represented the antithesis of fashion – and start incorporating their styles into high-end fashion. The same happened with respect to non-Western cultures, whose styles and patterns became desirable and inspirational to Western designers with the advent of mass travel and an ever-increasing desire for novelty. This did not eliminate the downward spread of fashion as set out above, but instead added an upward and sideways movement of styles. This, of course, challenged the

Opposite *Freed from the constraints of corsets, women's fashion in the second half of the twentieth century meant clothing could finally become comfortable as well as practical: a new expression of femininity.*

Top *Machinists at the Thomas Brown & Sons clothing factory, Brisbane, 1946.*

Above *Prada, the luxury Italian fashion house, was founded in Milan over a century ago. It continues to be run by members of the founding family and is recognised worldwide for simple, elegant designs from off-the-peg clothing to luggage, shoes, eyewear and perfume.*

issue of the originator of a design, as cultural 'borrowing' (or 'stealing') became increasingly prevalent in high fashion. While the origins of a design thereby became blurred, it is interesting to see that it still needed, and arguably still needs, the approval of the high-end designer to transform it from street style or traditional costume into fashion. The originator could now also perform the role of interpreter.

It is no coincidence that at exactly the same time, Haute Couture, and indeed Paris itself – the near-unchallenged arbiters of taste and luxury – were seeing their crown contested by new emerging fashion centres, and, most importantly, high-end ready-to-wear designers. The latter realised that conspicuous luxury and endless fittings were no longer in line with the new ideas emerging around class and gender roles in the post-war world. The new designers and fashion companies did not kill off Haute Couture (it survives to this day) – rather, they widened the fashion landscape and diversified our understanding and the very definition of fashion.

Once designer brands ventured into ready-to-wear, the concept of originality had to be reconsidered, as now identical products were sold to more than one customer; this meant that originality no longer resided in the uniqueness of each finished product but was increasingly understood as a concept that designers expressed through the innovative qualities presented in their collections.

Fashion's definition has thus seemingly changed profoundly since Worth's day, and yet in many ways it has remained the same: Fashion with a capital F is still elitist, only our definition of the elite has changed beyond recognition. Royalty, who were the fashion celebrities of the nineteenth century, have mostly become obsolete in the fashion stakes, and have been replaced by celebrities often famous for little more than simply being visible.

Fashion is still about novelty and continual renewal, only the rate at which this cycle plays out has continued to speed up, to the point where the very notion of a fashion season is now almost completely removed from its previous link to the actual calendar seasons. Fashion is still about authorship and the originating of styles, but our definition of originality has had to be widened, given how we increasingly use the old to create the new. Interpretation of existing raw material is now the key to how we understand novelty and innovation. Haute Couture still exists, but is no longer the arbiter of taste; that role has passed to the luxury ready-to-wear brands which continue to hold in place the self-perpetuating system of distinction, aspiration and emulation that drives fashion.

The definition of fashion set out above will guide the development and discussion of this book. Its focus will be on high fashion, and each chapter will look at the significant stylistic changes that occurred in the decade in question, and place these in their cultural and political context. For each decade, three designers who made their mark on fashion will be discussed, as well as three key looks. Some of the designers may come as a surprise – I have chosen to focus on individuals who, either through their designs or their business practices, best represent their times.

Opposite *Once the privilege of the wealthy few, fashion has changed from bespoke items tailored to fit an individual's particular frame to mass-produced, ready-to-wear clothing in standardised sizes and on sale in every major city in the world.*

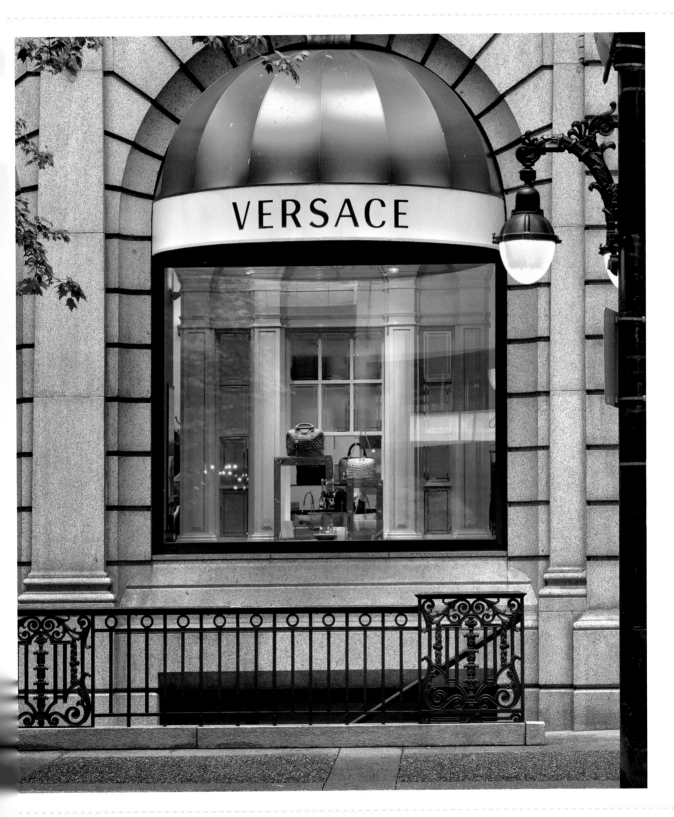

Timeline

◄ Informal yet stylish, the tea gown offered the Edwardian woman some afternoon relief from her corset in the privacy of her own home, or that of close friends.

▸ Paris celebrated the vogue for all things Oriental in fashion design, from evening gowns and opera coats to turbans and harem pants.

▸ Outside the home, Edwardian women always wore hats that were often oversized and lavishly decorated.

◄ Coco Chanel was first to spot the trend for clothing the idle rich by using everyday jersey to make chic suits that partnered comfort with luxury.

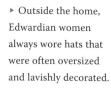

◄ A straighter, more tubular silhouette was achieved by a tunic over a long skirt to emphasise the vertical lines and minimise the hips.

▸ Tunic dresses became fashionable during World War One, worn without cumbersome petticoats or other undergarments. The simple shape required little fabric and provided the basic pattern that altered little during the following decade.

▸ Chanel defined Twenties fashion with her Little Black Dress, the embodiment of freedom, movement, relaxed morals and etiquette that marked the decade.

▸ The lingerie dress was popular in Europe and North America for genteel outdoor pursuits such as promenading, boating or a day at the races.

1900

1910

1920

▸ The contoured look returned, notably in Vionnet's bias cut which emphasised the draping qualities of fabric, literally sculpting the body.

◂ Paris under Occupation meant that avant-garde American designers rose to the fore, among them Charles James.

▾ Christian Dior's post-war response was the Corolle and his ideal hourglass shape.

he Jazz Age saw e shoulders and become part of fashionable look.

he Flapper Girl the epitome of enties fashion as nlines were hiked for dancing and ny beading caught eye.

▴ Film stars were also fashion icons and styles with accentuated shoulders were a constant feature of the Thirties.

Dresses hung from shoulder and emphasised the dy as well as orded greater se of movement.

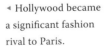

◂ Hollywood became a significant fashion rival to Paris.

1930

1940

◄ Chanel once again married comfort and luxury with her matching wool-tweed suits that defied the corsetry used in Dior's 'New Look'.

▲ Sixties chic looked to Pop Art, psychedelia and street style.

◄ Saint Laurent opened his ready-to-wear boutique and changed the nature of high fashion.

▲ The Seventies sought sartorial inspiration in the past, rejecting modernity in favour of retro glamour.

► Elegant daywear and separates were heavily promoted by Haute Couture and ready-to-wear designers alike.

► The Prairie or Milkmaid look represented a nostal for simpler times during the decade's economic downturn

◄ Couture designers including Balmain marked the end of war-time rationing and austerity with a return to femininity and opulence.

► Dior's cocktail dress was the shape of the decade: and Fifties couture experienced a golden age.

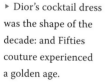

▲ The mini was born in the Sixties, and fabrics such as paper, plastic and metal entered fashion.

◄ Twiggy was the face of the Sixties: the look was short and sexy.

1950

1960

1970

‍o single fashion
‍ninated the decade:
‍is, midis, maxis
‍ trousers happily
‍existed.

‍Comfortable
‍erican Disco looks
‍e popular both on
‍ off the dancefloor.

▸ Excess and luxury
were key to fashion
in the Eighties.

▸ The Success or
Power Suit became the
dress code of choice in
the corporate world,
reflecting women's
increased involvement
in employment at
senior levels.

◂ Sartorial sex and
gender-bending was
the post-modern
Haute Couture
response of Gaultier.

▴ Versace linked
fashion and celebrity
culture to considerable
success, making him
a household name.

◂ Minimalism marked
a move to comfort and
understated luxury.

▸ Many new designers
proposed strong
feminine styles in
response to increasing
feminist debate during
the decade.

1980

1990

1900s

The 1900s were the golden era of Haute Couture in France, the start of a new century and the decade in which fashion shook off its nineteenth-century hangover and laid the foundations for modern fashion design.

By the turn of the century, Haute Couture had developed into an extremely well-organised and culturally important system that had two faces: the artistic and the financial. It was a business that dealt in exquisite luxury, extravagant design, high-end craftsmanship and artistic flights of fancy – but a business nonetheless, and one that was vital to the French economy.

Paris had been considered the centre of good taste and luxury since the seventeenth century, and by the start of the twentieth century its reputation was known the world over. The designs of the leading couturiers were reproduced in fashion periodicals across the globe, and their names became synonymous with quality and good taste. Fashion was created and defined by Paris and Paris alone; the adjective 'Parisian' had become shorthand for luxury, novelty and beauty.

Twice a year, ladies would travel to the city from around the world to order their new outfits from the greats of the day: Worth, Callot Sœurs, Jeanne Paquin, Raudnitz & Cie, Jacques Doucet, Redfern and the newly opened Maison Dœuillet. Their orders tended to be extensive and often ran into multiple outfits, as the fashionable lady of the era was required to change outfits several times a day, in line with prevailing etiquette. To be seen as fashionable affirmed a lady's good breeding, her status, her manners and, of course, her father's or husband's wealth.

An Outfit for Every Occasion

In the morning, a woman would dress in the first of her day outfits, usually a high-necked blouse worn over a gored, tailored skirt, accompanied by a matching jacket, a Redfern speciality. After lunch, an afternoon dress or ensemble would be worn. The silhouette resembled an upside-down lily: tightly waisted floor-length skirts that widened at the calves, often featuring lace panels and/or ruffles, were topped with high-collared lacework blouses. Dresses with similar silhouettes came in a variety of dainty patterned fabrics, often featured lace or cutwork, and were regularly worn with sashes. Favoured materials were light cotton, lace, chiffon, net and silk in feminine colours of pale pinks, yellows, blues and white. Trims, panels and embroidery were used in profusion, yet the outfits retained an air of elegance, femininity and weightlessness, owing to the delicate nature of the materials and craftsmanship. Thanks to their abundance of trims and decorations, these gowns were often referred to as 'lingerie dresses'.

Under their elaborate garments women of fashion wore petticoats (underskirts) and the S-bend corsets that produced wasp waists and what is often described as a 'kangaroo' stance, by pushing the bust forwards and the hips and bottom backwards. The corset also created a 'monobosom' by tightly squeezing the breasts together, resulting in a protruding 'pigeon bust'.

Left *Edwardian fashion was a tour de force in terms of craftsmanship. Elaborate evening dresses featured a combination of embroidery, lace, elaborate edging and silk flowers. Light materials such as silk, tulle, gauze and satin were layered or had delicate lace panels; ruffles were used on skirts and sleeves. The full effect was frothy and feminine but also a clear marker of wealth and status. The delicacy of the work meant that much time and effort went into creating these garments; to be able to afford the time of others is a great luxury and at the core of the Haute Couture industry.*

1900s

By late afternoon, a tea gown offered women some temporary relief and comfort. The tea gown was an informal yet highly stylish garment that had become popular in the latter decades of the nineteenth century. Described as a hybrid between a wrapper (a robe) and a ball dress, the tea gown was designed to be worn without a corset, in the privacy of one's own home. It often featured an Empire-line silhouette, or consisted of a robe and undergown combination; both these approaches eliminated the need for a corset. Materials used for tea gowns were lavish, and these outfits typically had exquisite embroidery, lace panels or beading; the robes frequently had ruffles. By 1900 the rules were becoming more relaxed, and the tea gown was being worn by a growing number of ladies for dinner in their own homes or those of close friends.

For more formal evening occasions, a more structured evening gown, worn over a corset, was required. The silhouette of these gowns was similar to that of the afternoon dress, but the high collar was done away with, and the outfit instead featured a lower bustline. Evening gowns came in sumptuous materials, richly decorated in a wide variety of colours from the palest pinks to midnight blues. The look was topped off with extravagant coiffures, enhanced with artificial hair and a hat or hair ornament, such as embellished tortoiseshell hair combs or exotic bird wings.

Right *A flounced and richly decorated lace tea gown by English couturier John Redfern marked a departure from the tightly waisted morning dress, allowing women to relax in the privacy of their homes without the discomfort of a corset.*

Magnificent Millinery

Hats often took on epic proportions and practically dwarfed a lady's face and body. Like dresses and blouses, hats were richly decorated with bows, silk flowers, ruffled ribbons, net, feathers and even entire taxidermic birds. Indeed, some of the most exotic bird species were brought to the brink of extinction in the name of fashion.

European hat designs during the 1900s continued to favour broad brims and deep crowns with the full hairstyle that came to be known as Gibson Girl hair. Gibson Girls were named after the pen-and-ink illustrations by American illustrator Charles Dana Gibson, depicting the personification of the feminine ideal of physical attractiveness.

Shrugging Off the Corset

The frothy creature who defined the opening years of the decade was in stark contrast to the one that closed it. By 1909, the curved, pigeon-breasted, hourglass silhouette had been replaced by one with a much more vertical accent, and the waistline had shifted upwards and settled underneath the bust, reminiscent of French Directoire (1795–99) fashions. The colour palette had become bolder, and exotic influences and embellishments were now favoured over the dainty embroidered nets and intricate laces so popular at the outset of the decade.

This radical change is often presented as a fashion revolution due to the genius of one man, Monsieur Paul Poiret; however, fashion rarely works like that. Fashion is not created in an ivory tower: it is inherently social, and therefore any revolution is the result of many factors and many people.

Above *French couturier Paul Poiret.*

1900s

Above *The dancer Isadora Duncan shocked and delighted audiences with her natural, athletic form, unfettered by corsetry. In his many sketches of her performances Abraham Walkowitz, a fellow American, immortalised her thoroughly modern interpretation.*

Opposite top *The chiton was favoured by men and women alike in ancient Greece. This draped loose-fitting tunic inspired couturiers to dispense with restrictive undergarments.*

Opposite bottom *Margaine-Lacroix's figure-hugging gowns, split to the knee to ease movement of their wearers, caused uproar among race-goers at Longchamp, Paris.*

Poiret had trained with both Doucet and Worth before establishing his own house in 1903. The simplicity of his designs set him apart from the more traditional houses. He was no great fan of the prevailing silhouette and soon began designing outfits that did away with petticoats and, later, the S-bend corset. He proposed fashions inspired by Japanese cutting techniques, reform dress (see page 37) and the Greek chiton.

However, while Poiret undeniably had a profound impact on the decade's changes, he was not the only one proposing and experimenting with these new design approaches. His reputation as a fashion revolutionary was due in equal part to his innovations and his genius at marketing and self-promotion.

Callot Sœurs were in fact one of the first houses to start offering 'respectable' dresses that could be worn without a corset (or with a less restrictive corset), and by 1905 Paquin also offered more relaxed silhouettes. The popularity of the avant-garde dancer Isadora Duncan, who attracted praise and criticism alike for her new, natural style of ballet, cannot be ignored in this development; Duncan performed uncorseted in sheath and tunic dresses inspired by Greek and Roman costume. Madeleine Vionnet, who was head seamstress at Callot and would go on to open her own house in 1912, was particularly inspired by Duncan's freed body to create draped gowns that favoured mobility and fluidity.

The Callot sisters were equally important in popularising exotic fashion elements; they were pioneers in looking beyond the West for design inspiration. Throughout their career they experimented with dress cuts inspired by saris and djellabas, kimono sleeves, Oriental embroideries and, later, metallic fabrics. Like Poiret, their interest in non-Western, less structured garments contributed to the alternatives explored throughout the decade.

Another key name in the abandonment of the S-bend corset is Jeanne Margaine-Lacroix; overlooked or forgotten by many fashion historians, she was one of the most commercially successful couturiers of the decade. Her Sylphide dresses, presented as early as 1899 and inspired by ancient Greek costume, were designed to be worn without the S-bend corset. Instead, she created matching Sylphide corsets, often in innovative materials such as leather or knitted silk, that were far less restrictive, more elastic and less heavily boned. Her designs perfectly married reform dress and high fashion, and show her as one of the earliest, if not *the* earliest, fashion pioneer in the fight against restrictive undergarments and the promotion of a more fluid, natural silhouette. In 1908 she sent her models to the Longchamp races wearing her most exaggerated version of the dress yet, and caused a worldwide press furore. The fluid, bias-cut, body-hugging dresses were so closely fitted to the body that not even a sheet of paper, let alone a corset or a petticoat, could come between body and dress.

Not only does Margaine-Lacroix deserve credit for her contribution to the abandonment of constricting undergarments, but her 1908 dresses also helped launch the popularity of another radical fashion change: the return to a Directoire line.

The Directoire fashions of the late eighteenth century were characterised by a high waistline and vertical, clinging dress skirts. The straight silhouette needed no extensive corseting to shape the stomach, back or hips, as the 1908 Margaine-Lacroix designs had shown.

Certain other couturiers, including Paquin, Lucile, Callot Sœurs, Poiret, Redfern and even the conservative house of Worth, had already hinted at a straighter silhouette in some of their designs prior to 1908, but the press attention dedicated to the 'scandalous' creations of Margaine-Lacroix saw a hint transformed into a full-blown fashion furore overnight.

1900s

Poiret and the Straight Silhouette

The couturier most readily associated with this new stylistic line is arguably Paul Poiret. Not only did he adopt it in the majority of his designs from 1908 onwards, but unlike Margaine-Lacroix, who presented her dresses in pale, old-fashioned, tasteful hues, Poiret started opting for more striking jewel tones, inspired by Fauvist art, which had caused a stir at the Paris Salon d'Automne in 1905. It was Poiret's use of colour and later his Oriental detailing, combined with his love for self-aggrandisement, that cast him in the role of sole instigator of change, when in fact many played their part.

Another early promoter of the vertical, unconstructed line who deserves mention was the Venice-based Spanish fashion designer Mariano Fortuny. In 1907, he created his finely pleated silk Delphos dress in a variety of luminous hues; it was embroidered with Murano glass beads on the side hems to weigh down the lightweight silk. The design of the dress was based on historic costume and, more specifically, on the Greek chiton, which inspired and was interpreted by so many designers who were trying to usher in a straighter, more slender silhouette. His Delphos and later his Peplos dress, a variation of the former that closely resembled its ancient Greek namesake, were intended as informal wear akin to the tea gown, but were nevertheless adopted in more bohemian and artistic circles both inside and outside the home, and on the stage by avant-garde performers.

Poiret, who claimed that his bright colour palette in the closing years of the decade was inspired by art, was probably equally influenced by Fortuny, whose gowns he imported as early as 1908, a mere year after their inception and, of course, the very year in which the vertical silhouette took hold in fashion.

By 1909 the new line had become established and all those who prayed at the altar of high fashion, except for the very conservative or very old, had abandoned the unnecessarily fussy and restrictive fashions of earlier years. This is not to say that the corset disappeared entirely; this straight line certainly called for less of the

Opposite *Early Lanvin outfit consisting of a tunic worn over a long skirt. The silhouette was designed to be worn without an S-bend corset and shows the shift towards a straighter, tubular shape in fashion. The hips are de-emphasised through the vertical lines of the skirt and the tunic. Date unknown, c. 1910–13.*

Left *Mariano Fortuny's extraordinary textiles referenced old Venetian and Arabian influences and became hugely popular for their brilliant colours and versatility. Elegant yet comfortable, his Delphos gown, designed in 1907 and produced in fine, pleated silk, hugged the body and shimmered like the skin of a snake.*

body to be tightly laced up, but only the very slender, daring and young abandoned their stays altogether. What took their place was a variety of elasticated corsets and corselets that flattened rather than enhanced natural features. Although these were certainly more comfortable, we should not exaggerate the degree of body liberation which is often attributed to these new vertical fashions. That total liberation would have to wait a while yet.

However, huge leaps forward were made and the fashions at the end of the decade look astonishingly modern compared to those at the start. What is vital to recognise is that the innovations in cut that modernised fashion developed out of reinterpretations of historic dress. It was a case of looking backwards in order to move forwards.

In the space of less than eight years Parisian fashion, and thus global fashion, had presented a whole new silhouette that was more modern than any that had gone before, one that would lay the foundations for arguably the biggest change in twentieth-century fashion history: the alignment of fashion and comfort in women's dress.

Jeanne Paquin

Jeanne Paquin was a leading French Haute Couture designer who, after training at Parisian fashion house Rouff, opened her own maison in 1891, next door to Worth's, with the help of her businessman husband.

In 1900, she was chosen to be President of the Fashion Section for the Paris Universal International Exhibition and showed a range of spectacular evening gowns, modelling some herself. The house quickly became known for its innovative and forward-looking collections, and indeed Paquin made a significant contribution to the silhouette changes of the opening decade of the century; she was experimenting with straighter, at times uncorseted, silhouettes by 1905.

Paquin offered an extensive variety of designs to suit customers of all ages, but became specifically known for her eighteenth-century-style pastel-coloured evening dresses, romantic afternoon dresses, tailored day dresses and ensembles, and later her Oriental creations. Like Poiret, and later Lanvin and Chanel, she frequently collaborated with artists, illustrators, architects and stage designers, including Léon Bakst, Georges Barbier and Louis Süe (of Süe et Mare). During her career she created stage costumes (and dressed the great actresses and opera singers of the day) and designed interior decoration schemes for private residences.

Not only was Paquin a highly successful designer (employing up to 2,000 workers), she was also a business pioneer and opened branches of her house in London, Buenos Aires, New York and Madrid. Her genius for promotion saw her sending models wearing her designs to the races and the opera, where they were guaranteed to attract the attention of both the press and the beau monde.

In 1912, Paquin signed an exclusive contract with the elitist fashion publication *Gazette du Bon Ton* (see page 41) along with six other leading Paris designers of the day – Paul Poiret, Louise Chéruit, Georges Dœuillet, Jacques Doucet, Redfern & Sons, and the House of Worth – cementing her reputation as a luxury fashion innovator and 'artist of fashion'. This status was reflected by her client list, which included the queens of Belgium, Portugal and Spain; actresses such Liane de Pougy and La Belle Otero; and the wives of American tycoons such as the Astors, Vanderbilts, Rockefellers and Wanamakers. Paquin retired from the house in 1920 and died in 1936, though the house remained in operation until 1956, surviving both the upheavals of the Great Depression and World War Two.

Opposite *For the first three decades of the twentieth century, Jeanne Paquin commanded the attentions of a fashionable clientele, opening branches of the House of Paquin in London, New York, Madrid and Buenos Aires. Paquin's Bacchante dress (c. 1915) was evidence of her love for romantic theatricality.*

Above *Painting by Henri Gervex entitled Cinq Heures chez Paquin (5 o'clock at Paquin's), 1906. This artistic interpretation of Paquin's crowded salon depicts saleswomen (without hats) showing clients (with hats) samples from which they can choose their dress fabric. The painting evokes the salon as a space where the commercial, the artistic and the social collide.*

Jeanne Margaine-Lacroix

Jeanne Margaine-Lacroix was a Parisian Haute Couture designer whose name has largely been forgotten. Her salon operated from approximately 1889 to 1929.

By the opening decade of the twentieth century her name can be found in many of the better fashion publications, and she had an extensive and loyal clientele. Her success is affirmed by the fact that her shop interior on the Boulevard Haussmann was designed by that leading arbiter of taste Louis Süe, of Süe et Mare, whose commissions did not come cheap.

Her style appears to have been a variation of the latest 'line' executed in wearable colours and fabrics. In an article for *The New York Times* in 1912 entitled 'Do women like eccentric clothing?', Margaine-Lacroix set out the relationship between Haute Couture show pieces and what ladies actually purchased and wore, thus demonstrating her sound, realistic understanding of her market. She described how Paris presents extravagant and daring creations, but that these are essentially about ideas and that their role is to invite change; no 'woman of taste' would choose to wear them. Instead these 'peculiarities' are stripped of their bewildering eccentricities and modified to form the new fashion. These comments go a long way to explain why she was forgotten, as fashion historians have often preferred to focus on the spectacular exceptions instead of the more mundane rule.

Despite her realistic design ethos, Margaine-Lacroix's career was not without innovation – quite the opposite. Her most important contributions to fashion were her sheath dress, the Sylphide corset and the sinuously curved Sylphide dress. Like their creator's name, these garments have gone mostly unrecorded in fashion histories. However, while visual and material evidence of her legacy are scarce, descriptions of these garments provide evidence that it was Margaine-Lacroix, and not Poiret, as is commonly believed, who gained popular acceptance for the Empire line at the end of the opening decade of the twentieth century. In 1908, three models wearing her tight Empire-style gowns caused uproar when they attended the Longchamp racecourse. Their dresses were considered too shocking for the time, not least because they were split at the side as far as the knee (see page 23).

Margaine-Lacroix's commercial success and perfect mediation between her design innovation and her understanding of the commerce of fashion – in addition to her being a female pioneer in the field of Haute Couture – should have been sufficient to ensure her legacy. Instead, her absence from mainstream histories of fashion speaks volumes about the uneasy relationship between commercial success and credibility.

Above *A rare photograph of Jeanne Margaine-Lacroix with her daughters.*

Opposite *Margaine-Lacroix was a pioneer in developing dresses that could be worn without stiff corsetry. Instead she favoured undergarments made from knitted silk fabric with minimal boning that outlined the hips and thighs but that clung to and revealed the shape of the natural body instead of the corset.*

Maison Lucile

Maison Lucile, run by Lucy, Lady Duff-Gordon, was an international fashion house that operated between 1893 and 1923.

Born in London but raised in Ontario, Canada, Lucy Sutherland began working as a dressmaker to support herself and her daughter after a short-lived marriage to one James Stuart Wallace. She remarried in 1900, this time to Scottish landowner Sir Cosmo Duff-Gordon. She opened the first branch of Maison Lucile on Old Burlington Street in London's exclusive Mayfair district. Her creations soon attracted a wealthy and famous clientele and 'Lucile' herself soon became an 'It Girl' of the London social scene. Her clothes were quite different from those of the time, but it was her business sense that can be seen as revolutionary, when compared to that of her contemporaries. She had an eye for colour, and artfully blended muted tones to create romantic silhouettes; dresses made from sheer clinging chiffons or layers of diaphanous lace in nude tones were decorated with silk ribbons or flowers. She was among the first to name her creations, and opted for romantic or erotic titles (for what she called her Gowns of Emotion) such as 'Give Me Your Heart' and 'The Sighing Sound of Lips

Unsatisfied' – a practice comparable to the contemporary naming of perfume and make-up to sell the aura of attractiveness. It was her lingerie, however, that afforded her worldwide fame: her daring sheer and lace creations were highly sought after and she designed the wedding trousseaux of many celebrities and aristocrats.

She also created the Personality Dress, which she designed specifically to suit each client's character and cannily accessorised with bags, shoes and parasols. Lucile would spend hours, even days, with the women lucky enough to wear a personality dress, in order to capture the essence of their character, which she then transformed into a stunning gown – an ingenious way to cash in on her own fame and the self-importance of the elite. After a meeting with actress Ellen Terry she began designing stage costumes, which were so well received that they influenced fashion and extended her impressive list of international royalty and celebrity clients even further. Like Paquin, Lucile was one of the first global fashion brands, with branches in Paris, New York and Chicago. Her empire also included perfumes, cosmetics and accessories, and later a pioneering mail-order fashion line for Sears Roebuck.

Like several of her contemporaries, she experimented early on with silhouettes that abandoned the corset, and her popularisation of lingerie contributed to this shift. She was one of the first to hold 'mannequin parades' (along with Worth and Poiret), a practice that would grow into the modern-day fashion show.

The house fell into financial trouble after World War One as Lucile's romantic, fussy gowns now felt very out of touch with the new age, and it finally closed in 1923 when it went bankrupt.

Left *Lady Duff-Gordon (Lucile) was one of the passengers on the* Titantic's *fateful voyage in 1912. She was rescued, and provided a vivid account of her experience.*

Opposite *This opera cape with stylised rose design worn over a lace and silk dress are typical of how Lucile adapted the fashions of the moment and added her own personal, often romantic, twist.*

Hats

The opening decade of the twentieth century was still highly regulated by social etiquette norms. These described, if not dictated, appropriate behaviour for 'respectable' men and women, including directives on appropriate dress. One of the most central of these was the expectation that women should wear a hat when outside the home. Hats of varying size, shape and decoration had been fashionable throughout the previous centuries; however, in this period they took on proportions never seen before. Hats were a way for the wearer to show off her taste, status, wealth and individuality. Exuberant headgear was an essential element of fashion, and fashion magazines featured pages in every edition exclusively dedicated to the latest hat styles – a tradition now entirely lost.

Hats could be purchased off the peg, but ladies of status frequented high-end milliners and had theirs custom-made for a perfect fit. Milliners worked closely with both their clients and the Haute Couture designers, as their creations were meant to complement the colours, shapes and embellishments of the season. Thus, the elite milliners were based near the Haute Couture district in Paris both for their clients' convenience and so as to be close to where the 'New' originated.

● In 1900, hats came in a variety of sculpted forms and were decorated with ribbons, bows, artificial flowers, hatpins, feathers and, for those who could afford it, entire stuffed birds. The fashion for feathers had reached its pinnacle in the 1880s and 1890s, and was so extensive that bird protection leagues were founded in the USA and the UK as both domestic and exotic species were at serious risk of extinction due to fashion.

From 1903 onwards, day hats with wider brims were favoured. By 1905 a vogue for historic styles (in particular straw boaters and bonnets) was noticeable; these perfectly complemented the popular lingerie dresses.

● By 1907, hats were not merely wide but were also growing in height and taking on an oversized appearance. These enlarged cloche hats now sat over the head and no longer perched on top of it.

● Hats for evening wear followed the same fashion pattern but were even more excessively decorated than daywear styles. The exception was the turban, which in 1909 became popular owing to Poiret's and Paquin's Oriental designs but was never worn as a day style.

The Lingerie Dress

Also known as the afternoon or lawn dress

The lingerie dress reigned as the summer afternoon attire of choice for ladies in Europe and America throughout the decade. The shape and colour of these dresses bore a great resemblance to the chemise dress that had been popularised by Marie Antoinette in the late eighteenth century.

The lingerie dress was the norm at garden parties, at the races, on seaside promenades, at boating events and a host of other outings on the summer social calendar. The outfit was accessorised accordingly: for more formal social gatherings long gloves, lace parasols and elaborate matching hats were donned, while for less formal occasions such as games of croquet, lawn tennis or badminton a decorated straw boater was appropriate. The popularity of the lingerie dress was widespread and transcended class boundaries. Patterns for home dressmaking were available at very low cost, and the ready-to-wear versions available from Sears Roebuck in the USA were aimed at a general audience. However, for those with money to burn, only a Parisian original would do – lingerie dresses by Jacques Doucet and by Martial et Armand were particularly coveted, and the former created exquisite versions in floral-printed chiffons.

While the popularity of the lingerie dress spanned the decade, that is not to say that distinctive changes weren't introduced: the waistline, hemline, sleeves, but most importantly the cut of the silhouette, all changed in line with fashion.

____ Lingerie dresses at the start of the decade emphasised the bust, waist and hips, and had fuller, swirling skirts. Those at the decade's end were narrower and emphasised verticality through lace panel inserts and flat trimmings, instead of the excessive fluffy ruffles previously fashionable.

____ Normally white or pale pastel in colour, and made of lightweight fabrics such as muslin, voile, linen, batiste or cotton, lingerie dresses were elaborately trimmed with lace inserts and flounces, eyelet cotton, appliqué, ribbons, embroidery and ruffles. The dress on the right with its high collar, tight waist and decorated sleeves, bodice and skirt was the favoured fashionable afternoon wear for much of the decade.

⊕ Owing to the sheer nature of the fabrics used for these dresses, a camisole, petticoat or full slip was often worn underneath, or alternatively the dress was lined.

⊕ Although mostly referred to as dresses, these ensembles could also come as a skirt and matching blouse. Because these outfits were worn with sashes, one can't always distinguish between the two.

The Vertical Silhouette

Most fashion histories credit Paul Poiret with the introduction of the vertical line and consequently the abandonment of the S-bend corset, but however influential his contribution was to this shift, to credit him alone misses the importance of the change.

By 1907, a significant number of couture houses had included at least one dress in each collection that was formal yet could be worn without the S-bend corset (note that most were still worn with some form of supportive undergarment, as to go without entirely would be considered vulgar).

Callot Sœurs, Paquin, Poiret and Margaine-Lacroix had all hinted at a more vertical silhouette as early as 1903. While each designer's version was different in cut and execution, all shared a desire to liberate the female body. The two most important influences on their method for achieving this were the growing interest in Asian, and specifically Japanese, art and culture and the popularity of reform dress (garments suggested by dress reformers and artists who wanted to reform nineteenth-century fashion either for aesthetic but, more importantly, for health and comfort reasons) in artistic circles. The kimono, the traditional Japanese garment with a structured appearance yet without tailoring, was used as a blueprint by various couturiers to re-conceptualise and rethink their approaches to dressmaking; its influence is most clearly noted in Poiret's work, but is also discernible in that of Callot Sœurs, Fortuny, Lucile and even Maison Worth.

Particularly popular in artistic circles such as the Vienna Secession and the Arts and Crafts movement, reform dress came in various incarnations. Department stores such as Liberty (London), the Weiner Werkstätte showroom (Vienna) and Hermann Gerson (Berlin) sold these fashions, but it was through the support of Paul Poiret that they entered the realms of high fashion and that progressive ideas towards the female body became accepted by the mainstream.

—— Margaine-Lacroix's Sylphide dress represents the first extremely well-documented and popular style that was worn without an S-bend corset and was very much cut to emphasise verticality – so much so in fact that it clung tightly to the body.

⊕ Mariano Fortuny's Delphos dress was cut like a medieval T-tunic and hung straight down the body, the pleated silk emphasising its verticality, while Paul Poiret offered a variety of dresses, coats and tunics, all of which were cut to achieve a straight and nearly flat silhouette.

⊕ Since the mid-nineteenth century, the vertical silhouette had taken inspiration from the kimono in addition to medieval and ancient Greek costume. All of these shared flowing (often draped) lines that hung from the shoulders, avoided fussy tailoring and used the body to give shape to the garment rather than make the garment shape the body.

1910s

On 4 June 1910, the Ballets Russes, under the direction of Sergei Diaghilev, premiered *Scheherazade* at the Paris Opéra. The ballet, attended by the beau monde of Paris, depicted the erotic pairing of a Caucasian female with a black servant, and was to have a profound impact on art and fashion over the next four years.

The set and costumes, designed by Léon Bakst, were an Orientalist fantasy of colour, texture and a good dose of scandalous sexuality. In his costumes Bakst paired bright purples with luminous oranges, jonquil yellows with peacock blues, and dressed the dancers in diaphanous harem pants, bejewelled minaret tunics, turbans and long strings of pearls. The outrageous nature of the story, dance style and costumes ensured the ballet's immediate success – and its reimagining of Ottoman dress inspired leading couturiers to become more daring in their designs in an effort to remain of the moment.

Eastern Promise

The designer who aligned himself most closely to this new Orientalist vogue was Paul Poiret, who embraced the bold new colour schemes and successfully translated the stage costumes into the latest fashions. Both through shape and embellishment he infused his 1910 collection with an exotic feel: kimono-sleeved opera coats, harem pants paired with lampshade tunics, embroidered turbans... all executed in bright silks and sumptuous velvets with bold embroideries and prints.

A year later, he launched his first perfume and a cosmetics line, named Rosine after his first daughter, which came in minaret-shaped scent bottles; and

Above *Bakst's fantastical Oriental costumes inspired several couturiers, none more so than Paul Poiret.*

Left *Costume design by Léon Bakst for Rimsky-Korsakov's orchestral work* Scheherazade, *which was based on the Arab legend* One Thousand and One Nights.

a decorative arts company, named Martine after his second daughter, that sold Orientalist interior products and saw him become the first designer to offer a total lifestyle.

While he was unquestionably Orientalism's most famous, if not its most ardent, promoter, other Haute Couture houses were not left behind. Callot Sœurs saw this move to overt Orientalism as an opportunity to experiment further with more comfortable modern

shapes, and their creations now also often featured Moorish-style embellishments. Paquin also embraced the look wholeheartedly in her luxurious evening-wear offerings through asymmetrical draping, peplums and the pairing of shift dresses with *cache-cœur* (wrap) tunics. These latest fashions were complemented by oversized opera coats and wrap-around cloaks in heavy silk velvets with embroideries inspired by Chinese, Japanese and Moorish designs.

1910s

A More Down-to-Earth Approach

It is important to note that these indulgent Orientalist fantasies were mostly limited to evening wear – and that daywear, though it might include a hint of the exotic here or there, was on the whole less ostentatious and more sensible. Tailored walking suits in the newer, straighter line (also presented by Poiret) reflected women's increased social mobility (mirroring the steadily shifting political attitudes towards women) and those at the height of fashion were procured from Maison Redfern and Maison Chéruit.

Lingerie dresses continued to be appropriate afternoon wear, but also adopted the high-waisted Directoire silhouette. Excessive petticoats were shed in favour of a straighter tunic shape; though the more daring opted for bright colours, the heavily worked, white cotton lingerie dress remained a firm favourite.

The afternoon tea gown had mostly disappeared from women's wardrobes, but its influence nevertheless lived on. Pattern cutting in the opening years of the teens employed a lot of wrap-around, housecoat/kimono shapes, in particular for evening gowns and coats, and these forms can be directly traced back to earlier tea-gown styles.

While these garments gave women more physical freedom, the idea of body liberation is never quite as linear as we'd like to think; not long after Poiret's harem pants and tunic combo, he introduced the hobble skirt – a straight skirt that narrowed from the knees to the ankles, thereby shackling the wearer's legs and feet and literally making them hobble – to the endless amusement of the satirical press.

Haute Écriture

This tension between the exotic and the practical raises an interesting point when viewed in light of the luxury fashion publications available at the time, which then, as now, focused on the newest, latest and often most shocking, while largely ignoring the more subdued styles offered by couturiers for their older, more conservative clients.

A magazine instrumental in shaping the image of the fashions of this period was the *Gazette du Bon Ton* – 'the journal of good taste' – which was an extremely elitist, expensive publication made up of hand-tinted pochoir prints (fine, limited-edition stencil prints) executed by the leading artists and illustrators of the day. The magazine had exclusive contracts with seven of the top couture houses: Worth, Poiret, Redfern, Doucet, Chéruit, Paquin and Dœuillet. Catering to a wealthy, elitist market (a subscription that cost approximately £350 or $530 in today's money), it foregrounded the avant-garde and extraordinary rather than the everyday.

This selective representation of designs and designers meant that many of the decade's most prominent and successful couturiers were never featured in the publication, most notably Callot Sœurs, Lucile and, later in the decade, Chanel. The absence of these (and other) couturiers has in effect skewed fashion history, placing undue emphasis on certain names and styles. This raises the question: should fashion history be about recording the new and extravagant, or should it reflect what most Haute Couture clients actually purchased and, more importantly, what filtered down to and impacted on the masses?

LE SOIR TOMBE...
Robe du soir de Doucet

Opposite *Walking suits had been popular in previous decades but became* de rigueur *in the 1910s and represented one of the more practical ensembles in women's wardrobes.*

Above *The* Gazette du Bon Ton *set out to showcase the designs of top Parisian couture houses. This page features an evening gown by Jacques Doucet.*

End of an Era

Despite the efforts of magazines like the *Gazette du Bon Ton*, a convergence of 'real life' and the luxury bubble that was Haute Couture was soon to become a reality. In August 1914, the declaration of war initially had little impact on the course of Parisian collections, probably because, like the rest of the world, couturiers believed the war would be over by Christmas. (In the *Gazette du Bon Ton*, tiered afternoon skirts and dresses, peplums and walking costumes made up the majority of the content.) By 1915, however, when it had started to dawn on people that this wasn't going to be the easy victory they had predicted, a shift in tone had crept in.

Fashion histories tend to ascribe changes in style to the greater need for practicality, women's engagement in war work, rationing of certain fabrics and a more sombre mood – and for ordinary women this was very true. However, those who could afford Haute Couture were far less affected by the war, and while they certainly participated in voluntary 'work' to aid the war effort, this did not generally involve working in factories or canteens.

The couturiers' offerings did start to reflect the real world to the extent that their designs took on a more practical dimension through an increased emphasis on masculine tailoring, raised hemlines, and skirt and blouse combinations. In times of war, conspicuous displays of luxury by an elite are considered bad taste (and, more importantly, unpatriotic), and so less fanciful creations in more muted tones and fabrics were seen. Greys, browns, khaki and dark blues became favoured daywear colours, and tweed and wool became popular owing to their practical as well as durable nature. Military references were found in the tailoring of coats and jackets, and Maison Jenny's 1915 little grey suit embodied these shifts in the most fashionable of ways.

The most visibly radical change was witnessed in the rising of hemlines: the impractical, narrow pre-war skirts were replaced by a new, wider and shockingly shorter style named the 'war crinoline'. These round, wide dress-skirts were teamed with shoes and

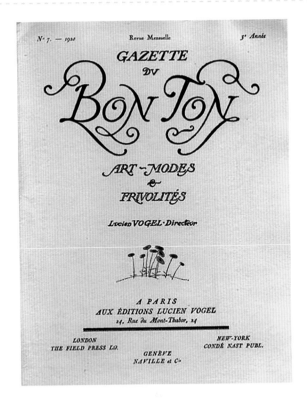

Above *Aimed squarely at the elite of Paris, the* Gazette du Bon Ton *proved highly influential, defining many new fashion trends between 1912 and 1925.*

calf-length spats to curb the moral outrage elicited by the sight of women's legs, which had not been publicly seen for decades.

The Coming of Coco

Arguably the most important change, which would have the most radical and lasting impact, was introduced by new kid on the Haute Couture block: Gabrielle 'Coco' Chanel. After a brief career in theatre design, Chanel established a millinery shop in 1910. Her success was immediate and she subsequently opened boutiques in the upmarket beach resorts of Deauville (1913) and Biarritz (1915); owing to its neutral status the latter had become the wartime playground for wealthy ex-pats who had left Paris to sit out the war in comfort. This was where Chanel launched her new design vision: the

The War Crinoline

The fashion for wider more voluminous skirts was dubbed the 'war crinoline' by the press, in reference to 1850s-style skirts and hoops. Interestingly, the fashion was a reaction to the wartime rationing and austerity but the fact that it was wasteful of fabric undoubtedly contributed to its limited lifespan.

Left *A walking or day costume with wide skirts and matching jacket by Lanvin, c. 1915.*

pairing of comfort with understated luxury. She did so both through her design and her fabric choices. She understood that her wealthy clients had little to do all day and were becoming increasingly interested in outdoor pursuits to combat their ennui. While men had an extensive sports wardrobe by this period, women's comfortable options were limited. Chanel remedied this by selling sportswear-inspired belted jackets, sailor blouses and her now iconic 'sweaters'. Jean Patou, who had opened the Maison Parry in 1912, had already shown a move in this design direction, but when his career was interrupted by the war (he was mobilised in August 1914 and spent the war serving in a Zouave regiment), Chanel was able to take the helm.

Left *Fashion illustrations were central to the Gazette du Bon Ton. Its founder, Lucien Vogel, drew on the talents of top Art Deco artists and illustrators who typically depicted the designs in context, rather than simply drawing models.*

Not only were her 'new' fashions less structured and tailored than those of her rivals, Chanel's use of jersey, a finely knitted, pliable fabric previously used for men's undergarments, meant that her clothes were elasticated and took on the shape of the wearer instead of shaping them. This use of jersey was truly revolutionary: Chanel managed to elevate a cheap fabric with no aspirations to luxury into the newest, most sought-after fashion. Her *pauvre de luxe* – 'luxurious poverty' (as Poiret bitterly described her style) – ushered in a new era of fashion, which saw a relaxation of form, material and attitude completely in line with developments in the real world.

Chanel was not so much an innovator as a translator; she understood that the old world order was being blown to pieces in the fields of Flanders and she matched her designs to the new ideas emerging around taste, class and femininity. She was vocal about the fact that her inspiration came from working folk, fishermen and the male wardrobe, and in a stylish but understated way she adapted their clothing into modern women's wear. Chanel's elevation of workwear and cheap fabrics into the highest echelons of fashion not only dispensed with pre-war Haute Couture ornamentation and fantastical design, but successfully married utility, comfort and fashion. She did not mould the body – instead, her oversized sweaters, jackets and skirts flattened it, and thus did away entirely with a need for corselets. Like several designers before her, she pushed forward the liberation of the female body and offered it the holy grail of fashion: comfort and luxury.

A New Beginning

By 1917, this need and desire for comfort, driven by changing definitions of luxury on the one hand and the changing circumstances of women on the other, saw the emergence of a less billowing, straighter, belted tunic line that sat above the ankle and ditched the cumbersome underskirts once and for all. This was the daywear silhouette that would see out the decade. With its simplified cut, Haute Couture fashions and those of ordinary women became more similar in shape than ever before. Haute Couture houses naturally continued to offer their clients extravagant evening wear, but even these elaborately decorated dresses became more tunic- or sack-like in shape and increasingly hung from the shoulders rather than being elaborately structured, setting the tone for the decade to come.

The exoticism that had characterised the first four years of the decade had mostly disappeared with the war and was now only to be found in surface decoration. The Directoire waistline favoured at the start had slowly moved downwards and waists had mostly settled in their natural place for daywear outfits, where they were accentuated by belts and sashes; some evening wear just about clung on to the high waistline, but the more avant-garde couturiers abandoned it and it became mostly a pre-war relic. While waistlines went down, hemlines had moved up and in so doing liberated the feet and ankles. The decade closed with fashion having adopted and incorporated the best ideas proposed during the war, often out of necessity, and carried them forward into times of peace.

Opposite *Coco Chanel in c. 1917 wearing a relaxed sportswear ensemble consisting of a skirt, a knitted jumper and belted cardigan. The three-piece suit made out of jersey was a true progressive fashion in that it combined comfort with style.*

Below *Covers of* Le Petit Echo de la Mode *published after the war show various tunic dresses and the diversity available in the style. Black was the predominant colour due to its associations with mourning; the high number of French casualties meant most families were affected and observed the tradition of wearing black.*

Paul Poiret

1913 Costumes Parisiens 99

*Petite robe de jardin, par Poiret, en crêpe de laine, bleu.
Fichu et poignets de lingerie.*

Paul Poiret was the leading light of Parisian Haute Couture in the first two decades of the twentieth century. He trained at the esteemed fashion houses of Chéruit, Doucet and Worth before opening his own house in 1903. From the outset, his clothes were characterised by a certain simplicity that was in stark contrast to the fashions of the time – indeed, at Worth he was specifically employed to create simpler daywear to balance out the extravagant evening silhouettes. Once designing under his own name, he continued to experiment not just with simplicity but with a more relaxed, at times unstructured, approach to dressmaking. He drew inspiration from the Japanese kimono to construct unfitted opera coats. He is often credited with introducing the straighter, vertical Empire silhouette in the first decade of the century but, as we

have seen, this radical change was not solely his doing, and neither was the abandonment of the S-bend corset. His contribution was nevertheless valuable. He was arguably the key player responsible for unleashing a fashion for fantastical Oriental design at the start of the decade. Shapes inspired by Japanese, Chinese and Moorish traditional dress can be clearly distinguished in his output from 1908 to 1914. He also decorated his clothes with Oriental embroideries and proposed jewelled turbans for evening wear.

While not the only one working in the Oriental mode, his colour palette was more vivacious than that of his competitors, partly inspired by his love of the Fauvist art of Henri Matisse and André Derain. By 1910, his star was on the rise and in the following years his empire was extended from fashion into furnishings and interiors. In 1911, he was the first Haute Couture designer to launch his own perfume line, although Lucile (not strictly 'haute', as she was not a member of the Chambre Syndicale) had started selling in-house perfumes as early as 1907. Regrettably, the popularity of Orientalist designs did not survive the war, and with the advent of simpler fashions Poiret's luxurious creations looked outdated by 1919. The house finally closed in 1929 and Poiret died in poverty.

His most famous designs include the harem trousers, the lampshade tunic, the sorbet dress and the hobble skirt. Though an innovative designer, his real genius and contribution to the modern fashion industry is to be found in his talent for marketing and promotion; his close work with artists and illustrators, which allowed him to raise the status of fashion; and his pioneering work in lifestyle retailing.

Above *Georges Barbier's depiction of a Poiret design for a garden dress, 1913. This wool crepe dress is a variation on earlier Poiret tunic styles.*

Opposite *Paul Poiret dominated dress design for the first two decades of the twentieth century: in America he was known as the 'king of fashion'; to his Parisian clients he was simply 'Le Magnifique', known for dispensing with the S-bend corset and introducing the brassière.*

Jacques Doucet

Jacques Doucet is often described as one of the great 'old masters' of fashion design. As early as 1817, his family established the House of Doucet in Paris, a business specialising in fine linens, lingerie and, later, ladies' apparel. From 1868, the reputation of the house flourished and attracted talented designers including Paul Poiret and Madeleine Vionnet, who both trained there. Jacques joined the family business in 1874 and specialised in laces and evening gowns. His design talents quickly attracted the attention of society ladies, actresses and *demi-mondaines* alike.

Doucet was especially popular with American clients, and by 1895 merchants from the USA were buying his models both to retail and copy, all of which contributed to making Doucet one of the biggest Parisian houses by the start of the twentieth century. Jacques Doucet was a fervent art collector and connoisseur, and his designs were often inspired by the eighteenth-century paintings he collected.

His romantic, luxurious but eminently wearable creations always had a feminine, elegant and airy feel. He worked in a palette of neutral pastels, often superimposing different colours to create a play of tones when the dress was in motion. He became particularly famous for his dresses made entirely of luxurious and costly gros point de Venise – a seventeenth-century Venetian lace characterised by large scrolling floral motifs. For decoration he favoured lace ruffles, silk ribbons, delicately dyed ostrich feathers, intricate beadwork and high-quality lace, again in muted tones. Though his dresses were among the best romantic and historic designs, he was not merely a designer trapped in the past – he also produced practical *tailleurs* (see page 53), which, alongside Redfern's, were some of the most desirable available. He was also an innovator in matters of fur, treating and manipulating it like fabric; his fitted fur coats were popular with women of all ages. Doucet knew his market and realised more mature women were not inclined to follow the latest fashion follies; hence his more conservative, romantic styles remained popular for most of the decade. But by the end of the war he shared the fate of so many: his work looked old-fashioned. Some younger silhouettes were introduced to the collection, and the loyal patronage of older costumers kept the house open for several more years, but by 1924 it was forced to merge with the smaller House of Dœuillet, which itself only survived until 1932.

Opposite *Art collector and fashion designer Jacques Doucet.*

Left *Doucet was known for his romantic and often historicist creations. While no great innovator, his attention to detail and his maison's reputation for craftsmanship made him one of the most financially successful couturiers of his generation. His more traditional offerings appealed to an older clientele who preferred more conservative opulence to the latest fashion fads.*

Coco Chanel

Gabrielle 'Coco' Chanel's career spanned from 1913 until her death in 1971. During this time she created many iconic pieces and her design ethos made an invaluable contribution to progressive ideas towards the liberation of the female body; she was the sartorial matriarch of modernity.

Coco's life was an extraordinary rags-to-riches tale, starting in a convent for orphaned girls in central France and ending in a private apartment at the Ritz in Paris. After an unsuccessful career as a singer, and a string of affairs with wealthy men which gave her access to the upper echelons of French society, Chanel became a licensed milliner in 1910, opening a shop on the rue Cambon named Chanel Modes. In 1913 she opened a boutique in Deauville (the seaside resort favoured by wealthy Parisians), which is where she introduced her luxury casual clothes made of fine jersey and tricot – fabrics almost exclusively used for male undergarments. The comfort these materials afforded, combined with her relaxed cut, resulted in a successful marriage of comfort and fashion, a rarity until then. Two years later she opened a boutique in Biarritz that was equally successful, and by 1919 she was registered as a couturière and opened her own salon, Maison Chanel.

Chanel made a significant impact over several decades of the twentieth century, but it was in the early 1910s that she introduced her first veritable fashion revolution – the combining of style, elegance and comfort – which underpinned her entire career and output.

Her style was radically different from that of her contemporaries, which set her apart and contributed to her immense and immediate success. She borrowed items and elements from both the male wardrobe and working-class dress, and favoured simplicity over vulgar excess; she was concerned with style, not fashion, and preferred classic, timeless pieces to constant change. A respect for the female body and a belief that women should be able to move freely was central to her oeuvre, and indeed all these qualities are found in her now-iconic pieces, including the LBD (Little Black Dress), the simple shift dress, a plain blouse, the leather quilted bag and the collarless bouclé tweed suit.

COSTUMES DE JERSEY
Modèles de Gabrielle Chanel (fig. 25), 238 et 239)

Opposite *Despite an inauspicious start in life, Chanel enjoyed acclaim and controversy throughout much of her adult life. Hers became the name associated with casual chic fashion and she went on to found one of the most famous brands of clothing and perfume of the twentieth century.*

Left *An early triumph for Chanel was to elevate jersey, an everyday knitted material used for underwear and sportswear, to the world of high fashion. Her matching suits were a hit with women who found themselves in holiday resorts sitting out the war. Their outdoor activities made comfort essential.*

The Tailleur

The *tailleur*, a made-to-measure women's walking suit comprising a jacket and matching skirt, was introduced to the fashionable wardrobe in the 1880s, but like so many fashions was derived from earlier garments, including eighteenth-century walking and riding habits. The *tailleur* was an example of the application of masculine tailoring techniques to the feminine wardrobe, or a feminisation of masculine dress. This gender borrowing was the main reason why the male press reacted with horror upon its introduction: it was perceived as an assault on masculinity and traditional gender divides.

However, women embraced these 'walking suits', as they offered a high degree of comfort and mobility. The British tailor John Redfern was their most famed and distinguished proponent, and a walking suit from Maison Redfern represented the height of good taste and luxury. Indeed, some sources suggest that Charles Poynter Redfern, who was in charge of Redfern's Paris branch, was the first to make a *tailleur*, around 1880, for the Princess of Wales.

The continued royal patronage of Maison Redfern (which had branches in London, Paris, Edinburgh and New York by the start of the twentieth century) meant that the *tailleur* and its creator's name were often featured in the press; this royal seal of approval for the suit for all manner of outdoor activities boosted its popularity significantly. Equally, the introduction of the vertical silhouette fuelled a desire for comfort and the *tailleur* offered women just that: it was the perfect combination of fashion and respectability without encumbering movement.

⊕ Classified as sportswear, the *tailleur* was worn for outings both in the city and to the countryside, and was a favourite for travel.

⊕ The jacket was derived from the male style and was made from tweed or high-quality wool in a traditional British hunting/outdoors palette of greys, dark blues, browns and greens; unlike its contemporary fashions, it was plain in cut and lacked ornamentation.

⊕ The increased use by women of public transport ('generation Metro', as Paquin described them), particularly after the outbreak of war, saw an increasingly practical reason for the *tailleur*'s widespread adoption: not only was it easy to travel in, it was also warm – a factor that was vital when fuel was rationed, which meant both less heating and less reliable public transport.

The Hobble Skirt

First introduced by Paul Poiret in 1908 for a select elite audience, the hobble skirt gained in popularity after 1910. It was named after the hobbling movements women made when wearing it, as it had the effect of shackling their feet.

Its youthful and elongating cut may have been perfectly in line with the fashionable silhouette, but for its wearer walking was difficult, getting into cars or onto public transport was seriously compromised, and descending stairs, stepping over street curbs and negotiating puddles were simply impossible. Women were often reduced to hopping or, worse, forced to lift up their skirts. The satirists had a field day: newspapers were filled with mocking cartoons, and there was an abundance of comedic postcards featuring women in hobble skirts trying to climb over stiles on country walks, getting out of punts or hopping like kangaroos.

Regardless of its complete impracticality, the hobble skirt became a fashion sensation and was particularly successful in America, where it was adopted by the masses. This was the result of both Poiret's popularity – by 1909 he was regarded as the 'king of fashion' – and the fact that the skirt was perfectly suited to mass production and hence available as an affordable ready-to-wear item.

—— The high-waisted, slim tubular skirt was tapered from the hips to the ankles – some had as little as a 30cm (12-inch) opening for the feet, while others had horizontal bands 'tying' the wearer's knees together.

● While Paul Poiret's versions were proposed in bright silks and velvets, some featuring striped or floral prints, off-the-peg hobble skirts were produced in a more subdued, wearable palette and a range of practical fabrics.

● The hobble skirt remained popular until the outbreak of war, when practical considerations surpassed fashion, but both the ready-to-wear and the couture versions did soon see the addition of kick and side pleats and back slits to facilitate movement.

LES MODES

Photo Talma.

ROBE D'APRÈS-MIDI, PAR REDFERN

The flat, T-shaped, belted tunic dress hung from the shoulders (that is, it lacked tailored structure) and resembled both medieval smocks and simple monastic robes.

The design can be considered as an evolution of the tea dress and a more practical version of Fortuny's Delphos dress; it also shared characteristics with various reform styles. All of these resemblances are an indication of its comfort.

Skirts ranged from the very straight (echoing the pre-war vertical line) to the rounded and full, seemingly a hangover from the wartime crinoline.

● The most common shape was fairly straight but often featured pleated side panels that allowed for a neat hang and ease of movement. The waist, which could sit under the bust – another pre-war throwback – or in its natural place, was accentuated with a sash or fabric belt.

The Tunic Dress

Also known as a shift or chemise dress

The tunic dress emerged as a fashion item during the war, and its cut and structure would remain the basis for fashionable dress for nearly a decade, yet its sartorial roots go back as far as the Middle Ages.

Tunics of varying lengths and shapes worn over skirts or harem trousers had been fashionable since 1910, but around 1917 the ankle-length tunic dress, worn without cumbersome petticoats or over other garments, became popular. Tunic dresses in various styles appeared on the pages of popular women's magazines, which featured dresses that ranged from richly decorated versions in embroidered silk with mesh sleeves for evening wear to plain cotton versions suitable for housework.

In the realm of Haute Couture, the Callot Sœurs produced exquisite versions in gold silk with Moorish embroidery designs and ingeniously cut versions in monochrome satins; both Chanel and Lanvin suggested luxurious yet practical daywear versions, again in a monochrome palette. Ready-to-wear producers relished the simplified pattern and the reduced amount of fabric needed in order to construct the dress. This may have influenced its development and popularity, as European nations were faced with fabric shortages.

The flat shape of the tunic dress altered little over the next eight years and became the blueprint for the sack dresses of the Twenties. While variations were introduced in regard to skirt length, shape and width, the basic pattern remained virtually unchanged.

1920s

In fashion terms, the Twenties had in many ways already begun by the end of World War Two, as the major silhouette changes that would come to define the Jazz Age were in fact introduced in the late teens. The tubular, tunic-like styles, loosely belted at the waist and with a raised hemline, which became popular towards the end of the war, already anticipated the dominant shapes of the Twenties.

The French couturière Jeanne Lanvin introduced the most popular of these tunic styles in the late teens; her *robe chemise* (shirt dress) was an unfitted, columnar dress that fell in a straight line to the ankle. She created this tubular dress as an alternative daywear silhouette to her famed, but often forgotten, *robe de style* evening line.

References to *robes de style* appear as early as 1912, but it was only in the Twenties that this dress, inspired by nineteenth-century styles of small waistlines, offset by crinolines and voluminous skirts, became the hallmark of Maison Lanvin. The early version of the dress adhered to the natural waistline; however, by 1919, it had started dropping below the natural waist. This dropped waist would be almost universally adopted for daywear (and widely used in evening wear) for most of the Twenties.

So the three major silhouette features of the decade's fashions – the raised hemline, the dropped waist and the straight, tubular shape – had been set in motion before the Roaring Twenties had even started. This does not mean that the line remained unchanged for the best part of ten years (hemlines rose and fell and waists at times disappeared altogether), but these changes were merely variations on and evolutions of those present at the outset.

Coloured by Culture

In terms of embellishment, this shape change also witnessed, and indeed allowed for, major innovation. The new, flatter and more angular silhouette became comparable to an artist's canvas for the creativity of Haute Couture designers and their exceptionally skilled workforce of *petites mains*, a veritable army of beaders and embroiderers.

Indeed, art and fashion became conflated at various points throughout the decade. The influence of abstract (and later surrealist) art made a major mark on surface decoration. Bold, angular and geometric patterns and shapes were used both for prints and embellishments by the leading houses; several couturiers collaborated with artists (notably Poiret with Raoul Dufy) and several artists (such as Sonia Delaunay and the constructivists Varvara Stepanova and Lyubov Popova) experimented with fashion. This rapprochement between art and fashion only served to elevate the cultural status of Haute Couture and to reinforce the similarities between the two creative fields.

Rober pour l'été 1920.

Top *An oil painting of Jeanne Lanvin, by the French painter Clémentine-Hélène Dufau, 1925.*

Above *Paul Poiret summer dresses, 1920, from the* Gazette du Bon Ton. *The various skirt styles that were fashionable at the time reveal a simplified silhouette and a preference for tunic-style ensembles.*

Above *Model wearing a Paquin beaded and feathered headdress, which captured perfectly the Twenties craze for the* style égyptien.

The influences on surface design did not end with modern art. The previous decade's flirting with Orientalism continued, but moved away from the all-out *One Thousand and One Nights* fantasies. There was now a more literal Oriental influence on the shape and decoration of garments: the unstructured, tubular, T-shaped or loose cut of djellabas, kaftans and tunics served as a direct inspiration for the Twenties sack dresses. The range of cultural borrowings now extended also to geometric Aztec and Japanese designs, tribal African and Native American details, Eastern European and Russian folk embroidery, Imperial Chinese motifs and Moorish-inspired patterns. These exotic influences were not limited to fashion: contemporary architecture drew from similar sources, highlighting the social and cultural nature of fashion but also showing its obsession with the latest and the newest.

Egyptomania

The most explicit example of this relationship between culture and fashion occurred in 1923, the year Howard Carter opened the sealed doorway to Tutankhamen's tomb. The spectacular nature of what he found inside enraptured the world and triggered a brief period of Egyptomania. Products ranging from Singer sewing machines to chocolate tins now came decorated with 'traditional' Egyptian columns and hieroglyphs. Not wishing to be left behind, and committed to their endless pursuit of newness, Parisian designers jumped on the bandwagon and Poiret, Lanvin, Vionnet, Callot Sœurs and many others presented capes, dresses and accessories decorated with Egyptian-style embroideries of lotus flowers, scarabs and a host of symbols and shapes inspired by the ancient world. To complete the look, Haute Couture milliner Suzanne Talbot created crown-like hats and luxury jewellery companies such as Cartier offered brooches, earrings and necklaces *en style égyptien*.

The Carter discovery also helped to further popularise the use of gold and silver embroidery and especially of lamé fabrics. The vogue for gold and in

particular silver threadwork predates the era, but in the Twenties became increasingly bold. The Callot sisters were early promoters of all-over gold or silver fabrics, and their shimmering lamé evening creations were coveted by ladies of fashion. Vionnet was equally a fan – her time spent at Callot Sœurs possibly explains why – and made many an evening dress in silver or gold that belied its exquisite and brilliant tailoring through its elegant simplicity.

Beading was also extraordinarily popular and was extensively used to create similar shimmering effects. Evening gowns could feature all-over beading, the quality of which offset the simpler cut; alternatively, more subtle scattered beading was utilised to catch the light when in motion.

Above *The cigarette-smoking, cocktail-drinking flappers scandalised the establishment and openly flouted Prohibition in the USA but aspects of their look appealed, albeit as a scaled-down version, to respectable women too – significantly because the dropped waist removed the need for a corset in favour of a simple bust bodice.*

Fashion for the New Woman

The idea of interplay between body and dress was central to Twenties fashions. The simplification of the cut meant that, unlike bygone fashions, these tunic or sack dresses that hung from the shoulders needed the body to animate them and literally give them shape. Their at times deceiving simplicity was very much in line with the ideas about femininity that emerged as a result of the war: the New Woman of the Twenties was a freer, younger, more visible and more active creature than previously witnessed. Her emergence was both a consequence of and a reaction to a variety of cultural factors, including the ongoing suffrage struggle, women's active role in war work, the sheer surplus of young women after the war, and most importantly the slow but certain disappearance of outdated moral and social norms and values. This New Woman was active and required a wardrobe to match her new status. The simpler lines that had been developing since the previous decade did the job.

The garment that has come to define the uniform of the Twenties New Woman is Chanel's Little Black Dress. Introduced in American *Vogue* in 1926, the LBD embodied new principles of freedom, movement and relaxed morals and etiquette. The simple black crepe dress was intended to be worn from morning right through till night, so doing away with the need for endless outfit changes. While its newness is often seen to reside in the use of the colour black, this is misleading. Despite the claims of so many historians and fashion journalists, Chanel was not the first to suggest black as a fashion

Above *Chanel's LBD remains a 'sort of uniform for all women of taste'. The transformation of black from 'widow's weeds' to the ideal colour for any occasion was compared by* Vogue *to the democratising appeal of the Ford automobile.*

The Not-So-New Woman

The years following World War One were a period of increasing independence among young Western women who marked their liberality by smoking cigarettes, driving cars and listening to jazz. Flapper girls, as they became known, flouted social and sexual norms. The flapper dress was sleeveless, straight-waisted and short enough to display a significant amount of leg clad in silk or rayon stockings when walking – or particularly when dancing – and flappers wore substantial heels. The look was typical of the reckless, independent, cocktail-drinking lifestyle popularised in the writing of writers such as F. Scott Fitzgerald and Anita Loos.

Left *Alice Joyce, one of the most popular film actresses during the Twenties, photographed by George Grantham Bain in 1926.*

colour – it had been part of the fashionable wardrobe since the nineteenth century. Neither was she the one who aligned it with fashion instead of mourning; this had also happened much earlier. She wasn't even the first to make high-fashion simple black dresses in the new style, as Poiret and several others had done so a few years earlier. The real innovation resided in the idea that a woman could wear one dress all day, for different engagements, and look elegant and fashionable for all.

A New Practicality

Chanel's LBD, like so many of her other fashions, was inspired by workwear (in this instance servant's uniforms), and thus offered great freedom of movement. Like her early designs in jersey, much of her Twenties fashion output struck the perfect balance between comfort and chic. Sportswear (fashionable outfits inspired by sporting outfits) was central to her collections and her commitment to these styles only increased their popularity.

Chanel successfully translated the new zeitgeist into her designs and others soon followed: 1922 saw many couturiers, including Jacques Heim, Jane Regny, Rochas, Schiaparelli, Hermès and Lanvin, all begin to create luxury sportswear. Lanvin, influenced by Brittany's regional dress, introduced a stylish Breton suit that consisted of a lightly gathered skirt worn with a short braided jacket and a sailor blouse. It became an instant success. Her sports-inspired fashions were in such demand among the rich and famous that by 1926 she was able to launch her sportswear line in Cannes, Biarritz and Paris.

Jean Patou, now back from the front, offered both 'real' sporting outfits and sportswear; as he dressed some of the most famous tennis players of the time, his popularity boomed alongside the rise in popularity of sports for women. His ski, tennis and swimwear was easily recognised from his initials that graced many of his creations. This can be taken an early example of logo culture: one literally wore one's taste and wealth on one's chest.

Chanel and Patou together were also responsible for another 'fashion great' of the Twenties: the knitted sweater-and-skirt suit. These suits, often accompanied by a matching belted cardigan, made for the perfect elegant yet understated, simple yet elitist day outfit, appropriate for city lunches, walks in the country,

seaside holidays, games of golf, cinema visits and informal dinners. Furthermore, the relatively simple construction meant that these styles trickled down to the lower classes, owing to the relative ease with which they could be copied by ready-to-wear manufacturers and keen home knitters.

In fact, at no time prior to the Twenties had the fashions of the elite and those of the lower classes looked so similar. The simplification of cut, in conjunction with the rise of cheaper ready-to-wear clothing and the emergence of man-made fabrics such as artificial silk, meant that for the first time in history all women except the very poorest could aspire to engage with fashionable dress. However, the similarity in silhouette did not mean that ready-to-wear and high-end fashion became indistinguishable. A dress might look simple, yet the pattern cutting could be highly complex (Vionnet being the best case in point),

Right *Suzanne Lenglen was a sporting icon in the Twenties. Her short, loose-fitting dress and trademark bandana gave the French tennis star complete agility on court and proved as much a talking point as her flamboyant, powerful game.*

Opposite *Jazz Age American dancer and actress Louise Brooks began the trend for women wearing their hair in a severely cropped boyish 'bob', which became part of the independent style of flapper girls with cloche hats, heavy make-up and short skirts.*

This new youthful look was completed by the latest hairstyle: the bob. Women cut their hair short for the first time in a century and this caused endless outrage, shock and scandal among the older conservative classes. The angular Louise Brooks bob was sported by the most daring, while others settled for the softer Clara Bow look. The whole package felt young, exciting and new, and those women protected by wealth and status adopted lifestyles to match: driving motor cars, dancing the latest crazes until the early hours, smoking – for those with money and the right credentials, life was indeed one big party.

and, while the cut of the more exclusive garments became less fussy, the fabrics used in Haute Couture remained extremely luxurious, sumptuous and, most importantly, expensive.

By the mid-Twenties this new, comfortable and youthful idea of luxury had become the norm for daywear, and even evening wear was visibly influenced by it. While evening gowns remained more ostentatious and overtly luxurious than daywear, their frothiness and excessive embellishment was toned down and their more intricate and complex shapes were simplified to mirror those of daywear. Aside from the wider social shifts, the Twenties craze for more energetic dancing played a significant part in this development.

The couture houses that did not keep up were losing business fast. Several couturiers were forced to scale down their operations and Callot Sœurs, unable or unwilling to adapt to this newer, simpler fashion, were forced to close.

However, by 1927 the first signs that the party was drawing to a close could be witnessed. Patou reinstated the waistline in its rightful place, lowered hemlines and adopted asymmetric cutting and skirt flounces; before too long, women's fashion started once again to feel more mature, and what in conservative circles was considered 'ladylike'. This new silhouette was still one that inspired ease of movement and shunned unnecessary embellishment, but it was altogether more grown-up than the flapper dresses that had been the norm only a few years earlier. This less angular, more traditionally feminine silhouette in retrospect signalled what lay ahead: the end of the blissful and youthful ignorance that had dominated the middle years of the decade. On 29 October 1929, the Wall Street Crash ensured that the party was well and truly over, and fashion would not escape its consequences.

Jean Patou

In 1924, Patou was the first fashion designer to create and employ a logo: the 'JP' monogram that adorned his sweaters and swimsuits was a visionary innovation, tapping into his clients' desire to show off their fashion and financial credentials. It was, arguably, the beginning of modern branding culture as we know it. That same year Patou began focusing on the US market, travelling to New York, where he found six professional models who returned with him to Paris to work in his salon. Soon after, he opened his Coin des Sports – a portion of his salon broken down into subsections dedicated to different sports. Here he sold outfits for pursuits such as swimming, skiing, aviation, riding, fishing, tennis, golf and yachting. These veritable sports outfits (as opposed to sportswear, which had a sportive comfortable feel but was not necessarily intended for physical exercise) proved such a success that in the same year he opened salons in both Biarritz and Deauville. He also launched his first line of perfumes, followed in 1928 by the first unisex perfume.

In 1927, with both the vogue for swimming and backless evening dresses in full swing, he launched a tanning oil, Huile de Chaldée, named after the ancient city in Babylonia, legendary for its amber-skinned beauties. The following year he dropped hemlines and returned the waist to its natural place, establishing the hallmarks of the fashionable silhouette in the following decades. The 1929 crash severely affected the house, and while perfume lines continued, clothing lines were scaled back. Patou's contribution, albeit brief, mirrors that of Chanel: each combined comfort, luxury and elegant design to create their own vision of a free young woman.

Jean Patou opened a small Parisian salon, Maison Parry, in 1912. His modern, simple designs, with an emphasis on comfort, were an immediate hit, but after two years he was forced to interrupt his career to serve in the French army during the war. In 1919 he launched his first couture collection under his own name which, like Chanel's, included jersey sweaters and comfortable clothing that freed women's bodies. These styles were an instant success. They fall very much under the sportswear banner, and the elite who spent their summers travelling to exotic locations and their winters on the slopes of exclusive ski resorts called upon him for their travelling wardrobes, while young Parisiennes adopted his jersey suits as modern designs for city life.

A couple of years later, Patou cemented his reputation as the go-to designer for sportswear when tennis star Suzanne Lenglen won at Wimbledon in a white Patou belted cardigan and pleated knee-length skirt.

Above *Three Patous and a Redfern silhouette (bottom right), 1925. While best known for sportswear, Patou evening wear was particularly favoured by a young clientele.*

Opposite *A Patou skiing outfit, c. 1929. The extension into veritable sportswear by several couturiers was a lucrative and clever business move, as it meant the travelling elite could now extend their brand loyalty to all aspects of their lifestyle to meet their travel and sporting needs.*

Callot Sœurs

Maison Callot Sœurs was opened in 1895 by four sisters: Marie Callot Gerber, Marthe Callot Bertrand, Regina Callot Tennyson-Chantrell and Joséphine Callot Crimont. They had no formal training, but had all been taught to sew by their mother, a lacemaker. Their initial designs utilised antique lace and ribbons to enhance blouses, but soon they started creating day and evening wear, and this was such a resounding success that by the turn of the century they were employing 600 workers.

In the early 1910s their clothes were perfectly in tune with the vogue for Orientalism, but aside from their extravagant evening wear they also continued to make pared-down versions for more conservative customers (often inspired by eighteenth-century dress), marrying the latest fashions with a timeless elegance.

They were among the first to use gold and silver lamé for dresses and their designs often featured exotic details – especially embroidery, the house's speciality. Callot Sœurs were known for their craftsmanship and their attention to detail, and they rightfully set a high standard in the industry.

In the opening decade of the new century they were pioneers in devising comfortable dresses that were designed to be worn without a corset. Their preference for unstructured garments (for which they often took inspiration from non-Western dress) made them fashion superstars in the Twenties when their simple, yet exquisitely cut and draped sheath dresses were coveted by elite customers. They often draped fabric directly on the body when creating patterns, and were promoters of bias cutting; indeed, the queen of the bias cut, Madeleine Vionnet – who trained at Callot Sœurs – claimed that her knowledge and success was down to the excellent and innovative instruction she received while at the maison.

The house expanded and opened branches in Nice, Biarritz, Buenos Aires and London, where it attracted the custom of royalty and society ladies. Aside from their richly decorated sheath evening dresses, they were especially known for their capes and capelets, and in 1920 they created the *manteau d'abbé* (priest's cape),

a short cape worn over coats and evening gowns that remained a fashion staple for nearly two decades.

During the first decade of the century their clothes were characterised by a tasteful palette of pastels, but by the Twenties they were using vivid Fauvist colours, often enhanced by the application of embroidery or beading. The sisters favoured gold and silver thread and sequins, particularly on evening wear, as they caught and reflected the light when the wearer was dancing.

By 1926 the popularity of the house had started to wane as their intricate and expensive creations failed to compete with the sportswear promoted by Chanel and Patou; the house was taken over by one of the sisters' sons and in 1937 merged with Maison Calvet.

Above *Callot Sœurs evening gown, c. 1920. This dress combines a richly beaded bodice with a straight skirt of floating bias-cut panels in a peony pattern brocade.*

Opposite *Evening gown of gold, metallic brocade with pearl and glass beads, 1921. This dress has all the characteristics of the Callot Sœurs: innovative pattern cutting, detailed and lavish embroidery and beadwork, luxurious metallic fabrics and a wearable adaptation/ interpretation of non-Western styles made them a favourite with the elite for several decades.*

Jeanne Lanvin

VENEZ DANSER

ROBE DU SOIR, DE JEANNE LANVIN

Nº 6 de la Gazette   Année 1921. — Planche 45

Jeanne Lanvin opened a millinery shop in Paris in 1890, after training at Maison Talbot. However, it was not her hats but the beautiful dresses that she created for her daughter that caught her clients' attention, and soon orders for matching mother and daughter outfits were flooding in. By 1909 Jeanne had abandoned millinery and become a member of the Chambre Syndicale, establishing herself as a luxury couturière. A few years later she created early versions of her *robe de style*, which would become her trademark. She launched her first perfume in 1917.

After the war Lanvin was one of the first to present comfortable chemises that had no darts, pleats or fitted seams; she attracted much praise for these throughout the Twenties. Like Chanel and Patou, she was interested in creating comfortable clothing, but her sportswear tended to be more elegant – her 1922 Breton suit, with its pleated skirt teamed with a short braided jacket embellished with gold buttons, perfectly exemplifies this. Lanvin's ladylike sportswear was so successful

that in 1926 she opened Lanvin offering sportswear collections in Cannes, Biarritz and Paris.

Aside from her sportswear line she had children's, lingerie, fur and interiors collections, all of which were highly successful. When in 1926 she opened a branch selling menswear, Lanvin became the first couture brand to dress the entire family.

Lanvin's contributions to fashion were many and varied but she is most remembered for her comfortable and wearable clothes executed in luxurious fabrics such as chiffon, lace, organza, silk, silk velvet, tulle, taffeta and satin. Her eye for colour was legendary: she bravely presented unusual colour combinations and developed her trademark Lanvin blue; she even opened her own dye-works in 1923. Her comfortable dresses were decorated with intricate and often large-scale embellishments including oversized cockades made of silk and velvet ribbon, large beaded bow embroideries, appliquéd silk flowers and petals, metal discs, clear and floral beads, tiny mirrors and coral.

The house took a serious hit after the 1929 Crash and was forced to lower its prices, but unlike so many others it managed to survive. After Jeanne's death in 1946 her daughter took over, and the house remains in operation today, making it the oldest fashion house in the world.

Above *An evening dress by Lanvin from the pages of the influential* Gazette du Bon Ton.

Opposite *Lanvin evening dress with sequinned cape jacket, belt and matching sequinned skull cap in gold lamé, photographed for the* Revue de la Femme *in March 1930.*

Le Style Russe

The Ballets Russes, under the direction of impresario Sergei Diaghilev, had taken Paris by storm in 1909 and their exotic fairytale-like stage sets and costumes had contributed to the vogue for Orientalism. This, however, was not the only Russian contribution to fashion at the time.

The 1917 Russian Revolution saw 150,000 Russian émigrés arrive in Paris, many of them from wealthy or aristocratic families. While some managed to bring their wealth to the city, many were forced, often for the first time, to work for a living. Their social status meant that few jobs were considered respectable or appropriate. Working for an elite fashion industry, either as designers or models, became a viable option for many, and several Russian couture houses, often specialising in fur or embroidery, started appearing.

Atelier Kitmir, founded by Grand Duchess Maria Pavlovna, specialised in traditional Russian embroidery and undertook work for Haute Couture houses including Chanel, for whom they embellished gowns, coats, shrugs and shawls. Maison Irfé, established by Princess Irina Romanova and Prince Felix Yousoupoff, opened in 1924 and was an immediate hit, helped by the beauty of Irena and the dubious reputation of Felix, who was rumoured to have been one of Rasputin's murderers. Maison Yteb opened in 1922 under the leadership of Mrs Buzzard, the daughter of Anne Lathrop of Detroit and the equerry of Tsar Nicholas II. All of the Russian houses and ateliers produced fashions in line with Parisian silhouettes but often added distinctly Russian elements.

◉ Le Style Russe introduced Paris to a new style of headdress: the *kokoshnik*, a traditional Russian diadem-shaped tiara, which, together with the cloche hat, would come to epitomise Twenties fashions.

◉ Taking their cue from the *kosovorotka*, a traditional embroidered men's tunic, the Russian houses created a distinctive garment for women that became extremely sought after.

Arguably the most lasting impact of Le Style Russe is to be found in the introduction of traditional fur and fabric combinations. Fur coats had enjoyed popularity for decades, but fur trims were hardly used until the Russian houses introduced a vogue for them on blouses, dresses and coats.

Sportswear

Models wearing knitted jersey skirt suits by Wilson's of Great Portland Street in London, c. 1925. The outfits are directly inspired by the styles of Chanel and Patou and the ease of wear they afforded saw them dubbed as sportswear. The geometric designs, also inspired by Patou especially, show the links between different creative disciplines; art, fashion and theatre produced a host of interesting and innovative collaborations during the decade.

— The sweater, a machine- or hand-knitted loose pullover worn over a skirt and sometimes accompanied by a matching belted cardigan, became iconic. It was versatile (it was appropriate for all manner of daytime social engagements) and its unfitted style allowed it to be worn without a corset.

— The use of jersey, a finely machine-knitted fabric, was indicative of the post-war interest in health and the emergence of the New Woman.

⊕ The decade's most famous and commercially successful examples of the sweater style include Patou's machine-knitted cubist designs and Schiaparelli's hand-knitted versions.

The Twenties witnessed the introduction of various garments best described as 'sportswear' – by far the most important type of attire to impact on women's lives during the decade. Items such as wool and cotton jersey sweaters, dresses, cardigans and coats all offered unprecedented comfort while not compromising on elegance. Initially reserved only for members of the elite, the influence of these types of clothes nevertheless trickled down to less well-off consumers, owing to the low cost of their mass manufacture and the simplicity of their cut. While the vogue for jerseys in a *sportif* style had started during World War One, largely thanks to Chanel and Patou, Haute Couture houses started offering increasingly more practical daywear silhouettes in the Twenties. Sportswear fitted both the fashionable silhouette and the new, less restrictive and regulated social climate perfectly. Their omnipresence in high-fashion collections gave these informal garments the Parisian seal of approval and their adoption was near-universal.

Owing to the relaxed societal norms introduced as a necessity during the war, women now had far greater freedoms in terms of participation in city life. This new freedom was represented in upmarket fashion magazines through illustrations of women driving cars, playing golf and even flying aeroplanes.

Schiaparelli's first sportswear collection (1927) consisted of sweaters in Armenian stitch and included her now-famed black design with a white trompe-l'œil bow motif around the neck. This item became so popular that she had to quickly hire more Armenian refugees for her atelier to keep up with demand. Its popularity was such that *Vogue* knitting magazines and a host of other cheaper pattern companies offered instructions on how to make your own, which allowed women of all classes to get their own Parisian look.

Robe de Style

The *robe de style* is mentioned in the French press as early as 1911, when the entertainer Mistinguett was photographed in a design by costume designer 'MarcieF'. The dress was characterised by a fitted bodice and wide skirts, and its historic roots date back to the seventeenth-century mantua. By 1915 the war crinoline styles had introduced a more widespread vogue for full-hooped skirts, but it was in the Twenties that the style really flourished and became an alternative to the straight-cut flapper evening dresses.

In 1924, *Vogue* stated that the *robe de style* had become Jeanne Lanvin's dress. While she was not the first nor the only exponent (most couturiers included a *robe de style* in their Twenties collections – notable were those by Worth and Callot Sœurs), hers were such a staple of the maison's output and were considered so innovative and tasteful by the press and clients, that they became her signature style. The names of her creations hinted at the dress's historic and cultural roots: designs such as 'Casanova', 'Dubarry' (named after Louis XV's mistress), 'Versailles' and 'la Malibran' (after a famous nineteenth-century mezzo-soprano) were featured in the luxury publications *Gazette du Bon Ton* and *Art, Goût, Beauté*.

By the late Twenties, the style's popularity waned due to the introduction of the new silhouette; however, its influence on future styles was considerable – it can be argued that the *robe de style* heralded Dior's 1947 New Look silhouette.

⊕ The Twenties' incarnation of the *robe de style* had full skirts and a dropped waist. The bodice could be either fitted or cut in the chemise style.

⊕ The fullness of the skirts was sometimes achieved through the use of petticoats, hoops or panniers, but could equally be achieved through clever cutting and the use of more rigid fabrics.

Jeanne Lanvin's *robe de style* of 1927 was silk moiré decorated with glass beads, pearls and metallic thread. It features the house style circular embroidery, found in varying sizes on many of the maison's evening gowns of the period. The embroidery and beading is executed with great care and detail and was equally a Lanvin hallmark. These luxurious and richly embellished dresses made Lanvin one of the most financially successful couturiers of the decade.

1930s

The Thirties are neatly framed between two major world events: the 1929 Wall Street Crash and, a decade later, the outbreak of World War Two. Due to this bookending – on the one hand a period of excess and on the other one of conflict and austerity – the decade does not always get the attention it deserves, and indeed is too often seen as a mere period of transition. This approach misses the importance and the transforming innovations of this period in fashion.

The Shape of Austerity

Recession is never a good time for experimentation, and so fashions tend to have a longer lifespan, as buying power is down and caution is at the forefront of the consumer's mind. In terms of silhouette, this meant that the waist would remain in its natural place for the duration of the decade, becoming more clearly 'nipped' from 1933 onwards. The natural waistline was accompanied by the highlighting of an Empire line through bolero jackets, capelets, shrugs and seams inserted just below the bust. Upper skirt yokes appeared for the first time, designed in a V-shape extending from one hip to the other, often clinging to the hips for evening wear. Skirts were often layered, tiered or ruffled, and at the bottom they tended to be pleated, panelled or gathered. These design features – accentuation of the waist, clinging at the hips and the lowered hemline – combined with the popularity of the bias cut to create a contoured silhouette.

Opposite *Screen print of two fashionable women, c. 1930. Both wear clothes in the new more 'mature' line that favoured lower hems and a natural waist. Thirties fashions accentuated the torso using various techniques including ruffles and bows as here. Smaller hats took over from the Twenties cloche as shown on the seated figure who wears a skull cap.*

1930s

Above *Madeleine Vionnet at work in her studio, c. 1920. She preferred to drape and pin directly onto the model and famously used dolls to make her trial garments using canvas (toile). This allowed Vionnet to create and figure out her complex patterns and perfect her draping.*

Moulded shoulders accompanied this focus on the hips. Italian designer Elsa Schiaparelli is often credited with changing the soft and floating 1920s shape to the more defined form of the 1930s by introducing this emphasis on the shoulders. She was indeed one of the first to use this silhouette in Haute Couture, but, as we have seen, designers are commonly the catalyst rather than the sole originators of change. These harder shoulders came in a wide variety: broad-shouldered tailored jackets, puffed, butterfly and banjo sleeves, and the use of ornate dress clips all served to draw attention to the upper body. The torso was further emphasised by lowered necklines that often came with wide, scalloped, ruffled and tiered collars, scarves incorporated into blouses and dresses, trompe-l'œil sweaters, bows, Ascot-style ties and corsages of fabric flowers.

A New Class

The day fashions of the 1930s saw the popularisation of the tailored and durable suit for women, which was a more grown-up version of the jersey suit of the 1920s that itself had matured into the 'ensemble' – matching skirts and blouses or dresses with coats. The practicality and versatility of the suit and the ensemble combined Twenties liberation (offered by sports fashions) with contemporary elegance. Durable fabrics such as cotton, linen, wools and velvet were favoured both in Haute Couture and ready-to-wear, demonstrating the total acceptance of the use of practical fabrics in luxury designs, which had been championed by Chanel since 1916. However, it should be noted that the elite did not abandon luxury fabrics – their options merely expanded to include the above.

For luxury floor-length, backless evening dresses, gold and silver lamé, satin and silk velvet were favoured. Fur of all kinds was worn both during the day and in the evening. Fur coats, capes, stoles and wraps were taken up in abundance. At the top end of the market sable, mink, chinchilla, Persian lamb, silver fox and a host of exotic monkeys and big-cat pelts graced the shoulders of the wealthy. The demand for luxury fur was such that several Haute Couture houses, such as Lanvin and Jacques Heim, opened separate branch salons that specialised only in fur creations.

The Imitation Game

Companies such as Sears in the USA and Littlewoods in the UK still took their design cues from Paris, reaffirming its status as fashion dictator. However, this system of domination was severely squeezed as a consequence of the economic recession. By the start of the decade it was well-established practice not only for individual clients, but also department-store owners and ready-to-wear manufacturers, to travel from the USA to Paris twice a year to purchase the latest styles from the leading couture houses. While the former bought for private use, the latter were there as part of the regulated and sanctioned Parisian copy trade.

Copying had been a part of the Haute Couture industry from its beginnings and, fully aware that imitation was inevitable, Parisian maisons sold official models for duplication in an attempt to regulate and indeed capitalise on this practice. This system meant that Parisian Haute Couture's seasonal stylistic changes were effectively filtered down throughout the fashion industry and around the globe.

Left *Fur fashion on the cover of French fashion magazine* Le Jardin des Modes *in 1934. Fur coats, shrugs and trims in a variety of pelts were highly fashionable throughout the decade. Hollywood's use of fur was in large part responsible for its revival.*

Colour in coat,
monogram, belt-
or heavy crêpe.
Fortnum & Mason

satin swimsuit
with "Lastex" yarn :
spotted Jersey wrap.
Lillywhites

Checks, small for
the suit, bookmaker large
for the coat, both in
the same Avon tweed.
Aquascutum race outfit

VOGUE 115

A Shock to the System

The couture house system, however, was severely shaken by the 1929 Crash. Americans were encouraged to buy 'local' through patriotic advertising campaigns in which fashion journalists and socialites endorsed US fashions to reinvigorate the economy. To limit the consumption of foreign goods, US import taxes were dramatically raised: for Parisian couture this tax could be as much as 90 per cent. These two factors, combined with the general economic downturn, saw a significant reduction in US clients.

Paris adapted in various ways. The most important and influential change was that couture houses were forced to drop their prices significantly. This price drop could only be achieved by reducing staff and producing less fussy and intricate creations that required less labour. This economic imperative constitutes an important but often overlooked factor in the silhouette changes of the decade and goes a long way to account for the absence of extensive beading and embroidery, so popular in the Twenties.

Another way to slash costs was through the introduction of 'semi-couture', which required only one or two fittings instead of four or more, and hence was much cheaper than traditional Haute Couture. Several houses, such as Patou, Schiaparelli and Lelong, increased their range of ready-to-wear items such as sweaters, and some couturiers even went so far as to offer mail-order and to use man-made fibres in their creations – two practices they borrowed from the mass-market, their supposed binary opposite.

Instead of offering radically different silhouettes each season, colour palettes fluctuated but shape remained largely unaltered. Instead, more noticeable changes in accessories – jackets, boleros, wraps and furs – were offered. This meant that those with smaller budgets would not be alienated nor look out of fashion if they did not purchase new gowns every season, and that instead they had the opportunity to update their wardrobes with less costly items.

Despite all Paris's efforts, many couturiers did not survive the decade; some of the 'greats', including Patou, Chéruit and Dœuillet, shut up shop.

Opposite *Fashion sketches for* Vogue *1935. Sports and daywear designs from Aquascutum, Fortnum & Mason and Lillywhites.*

Left *Publicity shot of Clara Bow for* Argentinean Magazine, *1934. The global reach of Thirties Hollywood cinema was central to it becoming a fashion force to challenge Paris. Not only were garments popularised by the stars of the silver screen, their styling (hair, make-up) was instrumental in creating the decade's beauty ideals.*

1930s

Above *Jean Harlow in a scene from* Dinner at Eight, *1933. Harlow wears a luxurious satin night gown trimmed in white fur. Boudoir scenes became popular in Thirties Hollywood cinema as they were a way to circumvent the puritanical Hays Code. They also allowed for the promotion of luxurious goods aimed at female cinema audiences as Hollywood was seen as vital to America's economic recovery following the 1929 Crash.*

The Silver Screen

Aside from the economic challenges Paris faced, another altogether different kind of influence also reared its head: a contender for Haute Couture's crown – Hollywood.

Hollywood both capitalised on the economic hardships of the Thirties and helped in trying to overcome them. While people's realities were often less than joyous, the cinematic output of Hollywood's Golden Age was characterised by lavish sets, glamorous stars and luxurious costumes in a bid to offer audiences a temporary escape from reality – the worse things got, the more sumptuous the productions became.

However, this excessive luxury was not just about escapism – it also played a vital part in the United States' economic recovery. Hollywood films were utilised as a tool to increase spending and strengthen the economy. Showcasing new products such as cars and white goods through product placement, and the creation of tie-in product lines, were two ways in which the film industry capitalised on its adoring fans. Fashion played a major part in this system, as it was generally accepted at the time that women were the major consumers of film and thus needed to be courted and enticed with the promise of spectacular costumes. Script departments developed what they termed 'fashion films', productions with scripts that favoured situations and stories that called for extravagant fashions; and publicity departments promoted these as 'fashion extravaganzas'. Alongside these fashion films, lines of clothes and dress patterns endorsed by the stars were created and sold through specialist shops and mail order so women could copy their favourite stars. Magazines such as *Filmfair* actively encouraged women to do so and offered star make-up and hair tutorials alongside mail-order fashions. Women had not only discovered a new, more democratic way to inform themselves about the latest fashions, they now also had an easier and cheaper route to access them.

Joining Forces

Parisian couturiers were on the whole appalled by Hollywood and declared its over-the-top fashions vulgar and cheap. Not only did Paris deplore the conspicuous excess, it deplored its accessibility, its popularity and thus its non-elitist nature. It would be wrong to think, however, that the two were entirely independent of each other. Hollywood took Parisian silhouettes and adapted and glamorised them through exaggeration. This was not just because of the aesthetic preferences of the costume designers – things had to be made bigger and bolder in order to make an impact on screen, as technology was not quite up to meticulous detail yet. Black-and-white film meant textures were more important than palette, and thus the use of feathers, fur and diamantés (mostly as jewellery) helped create tonal nuances that made up for what was lost in terms of colour.

Hollywood, and in particular American costume designer Adrian Adolph Greenberg (widely known simply as Adrian), is credited with introducing the Thirties fashion for bigger shoulders and leg-of-mutton sleeves. The hugely famous and popular Joan Crawford was dressed in accentuated shoulders by Adrian to balance out her supposedly 'manly' frame, but it does not follow that Hollywood invented this fashion; the story is not quite as straightforward as that. The essence of the matter is to be found in a quote by Lucien Lelong, one of the Haute Couture designers who had a less negative and more modern and realistic view on the subject of Hollywood. He stated that 'We, the couturiers, can no longer live without the cinema any more than the cinema can live without us. We corroborate each other's instinct.' The backless dress worn by Jean Harlow in *Dinner at Eight* was an immense hit and spawned endless copies; it was also very closely based on a dress created by French designer Madeleine Vionnet a few years earlier, whose impact at the time had been limited. So the relationship between Paris and Hollywood is that of creator and populariser, and the forward-thinking Lelong was right – the two corroborated and indeed needed each other.

The Glamour Fades

As the decade edged to a close, for all the accessible glamour of Hollywood and the elitist sophistication of Paris, neither could escape or ignore the reality of what was happening in the world. War was yet again brewing in Europe and, despite appeasement efforts, by 1938 the writing was on the wall. This sobering realisation was of course reflected in fashion, which took on less glamorous and more practical characteristics: hemlines went up, the ruffles and bows that had accentuated shoulders were stripped back and a squarer, more angular and masculine silhouette took its place.

Parisian couturiers, like politicians, tried to hope for the best and continued to deliver extravagant formal evening wear for their international customers; but clearly they were also preparing for the worst, as the designs of their daywear collections aimed at a domestic market proved. The 1938 Autumn/Winter collection proved to be a strange mix of luxurious evening gowns and practical separates for daywear. Even Hollywood, whose artifice had dominated the Thirties, toned down its extravagance and introduced a healthy dose of realism by putting its stars in comfortable trousers and blouse combinations. Fashions on both sides of the pond predicted the reality that was about to bite.

Madeleine Vionnet

Madeleine Vionnet trained with London dressmaker Kate Reily, Jacques Doucet and Callot Sœurs before opening her own fashion house in 1912. She was forced to close her business only two years later, due to the outbreak of war, and did not reopen until 1923. At this point she took over new premises on the Avenue Montaigne and opened her salon, which would become affectionately known as the Temple of Fashion.

Regardless of her patchy career, Vionnet became one of the most influential and respected designers of the inter-war period and is still cited today by many designers as one of the most important couturiers in history. Favouring a clear house vision over the latest fashion, Vionnet became known in her early years for her clean, sinuous lines inspired by Grecian costume, and in the Twenties as the 'queen of the bias cut'. Her designs eschewed corsetry, padding, stiffening and tailoring that distorted the female body – instead she used draping and bias cutting to enhance a woman's shape.

Her soft, flowing Grecian-style dresses were influenced by modern dance and in particular the avant-garde ballerina Isadora Duncan, whose dance costumes floated freely around her body and were worn – rather scandalously – without a corset. Vionnet admired Duncan's experimental performance style, and while at Doucet she made models show off the house's designs barefoot, just as Duncan performed – although this was considered too avant-garde by both Doucet and his customers.

Upon reopening her own house in 1923, Vionnet could fully express her own vision of femininity and found immediate fame and success; by 1925 she opened premises on Fifth Avenue in New York where she sold off-the-peg creations that were adapted to the customer.

Her unique vision combined with her exquisite and meticulous cut earned her the accolade of 'the architect among dressmakers'. Her deceptively simple styles in fact involved a lengthy process of cutting, draping and pinning – a process Vionnet executed on miniature dolls so that she was able to perfect the fabric folds. Her preferred fabrics were chiffon, crepe, gabardine, satin and silk; the latter two were particularly suited to bias cutting and draped perfectly to match a woman's natural curves and the fluidity of the body in motion. While she was not the first to use bias cutting – indeed, she spoke highly of her time with Callot Sœurs, who used the technique for coats and skirts, as instrumental in shaping her as a designer – she was the first to apply it to full-body dresses. It was these clinging gowns that secured her place among the couture elite, perfectly combining elegance, simplicity, comfort, sensuality and luxury. Vionnet closed her salon in 1939.

Above *In 1934, French magazine* Votre Beauté *featured a bias-cut Vionnet dress on its cover. The figure-hugging, linear quality is enhanced by the Empire waistline created through twisted fabric straps.*

Opposite *Model wearing a Grecian-inspired draped gown by Vionnet, made using bias-cut pleated panels, c. 1935.*

Elsa Schiaparelli

Elsa Schiaparelli was an Italian aristocrat who had no formal training in fashion construction, yet still managed to become one of the most prominent designers of the 1930s. After moving to Paris from New York, Schiaparelli opened a small fashion business with the encouragement of her friend Paul Poiret, whose uncorseted fashions she greatly admired. Despite favourable press reviews, however, the house closed in 1926.

The next year she launched a collection of luxury knitwear made with a double-layered stitch; these Armenian-stitch sweaters featured trompe-l'œil designs inspired by Surrealist art and proved an immediate hit. She expanded her range to include bathing suits, skiwear and simple sportswear dresses, and it was only in the early Thirties that she started designing evening wear and more formal daywear. Her chic yet wearable day silhouettes and her more avant-garde and experimental evening wear made for the perfect business combination, and soon Schiap (as she was known to friends) acquired her own salon on the Place Vendôme.

Her evening wear and accessories were often inspired by contemporary art, and she collaborated with both Salvador Dalí (Lobster dress, 1937 and Tear dress, 1938) and Jean Cocteau on some of her more iconic pieces. It was in these evening collections that her fanciful spirit came to the fore, often incorporating exquisite embroidery, experimental fabrics, new garment technologies and a bright and often clashing colour palette (she created her signature colour, shocking pink). Her experiments did lead to some problems: Diana Vreeland's dress melted at the dry-cleaners as the synthetic fibre was not suited to the chemicals. Schiaparelli was an early promoter of the zipper and, instead of concealing it, used it on sleeves, necklines or running across dresses as a decorative finish. She also favoured innovative and unusual buttons that included among many other designs crowns, insects, vegetables, ships, acrobats and musical instruments.

While she is now mostly remembered for these more artistic flights of fancy, her influence on daywear was and has remained significant. She was one of the first designers to present a wrap-dress (1930), a design that is aimed at flattering all body types and that has stood the test of time. She was equally instrumental in the Thirties vogue for accentuated, sculpted shoulders.

In 1940 she left for the USA, where she spent the war raising money for charity, and her salon was kept open by her staff to avoid German requisition. After the war she returned to a Paris now dominated by Dior, whose stiff, corseted silhouettes she opposed. The house struggled to adjust and in 1954 Schiap closed her salon, just as her arch-rival, Chanel, reopened hers.

Above *A silk and crepe evening ensemble by Schiaparelli in 1937, with metallic and silk thread to pick out a motif by the artist, playwright and writer Jean Cocteau.*

Opposite *Model wearing a Schiaparelli evening dress from c. 1934. It is an example of the contrasting, colours, fabrics and textures that were a hallmark of Schiaparelli's designs.*

Adrian

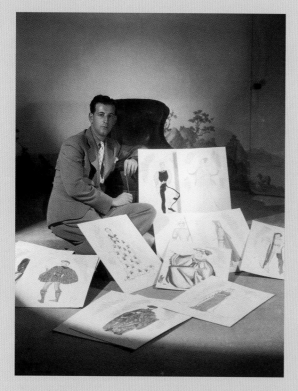

Adrian Adolph Greenberg, sometimes known as Gilbert Adrian but more commonly referred to simply as Adrian, was the chief costume designer for MGM (Metro-Goldwyn-Mayer) studios in the Thirties and dressed all its major female stars for the studios' productions. While technically a costume designer, his influence on fashion was considerable and his creations for the silver screen were extensively adapted for everyday wear.

Adrian studied at the New York School for Fine and Applied Arts (now Parsons), but soon transferred to their Paris campus. In 1928, after working for an independent studio, he was hired by MGM. Over the next decade he would work with Hollywood's biggest stars, including Greta Garbo, Katharine Hepburn, Jean Harlow and Joan Crawford.

Adrian was best known for his glamorous evening gowns and his personal interpretation of historic costume. Many of his film designs were adapted for retail, and dressmakers and ready-to-wear companies alike produced pared-down versions for American women. The star appeal of these dresses has often been cited as the reason for Adrian's success both on and off screen. While the fact that he dressed the most glamorous and aspirational women of Hollywood no doubt helped, it is unfair to suggest that his impact on fashion was merely by association. His 'daywear costumes', which have often been overlooked in favour of his more fantastical creations, show a great talent for pattern cutting, draping and design innovation.

While Hollywood costume designers were, to an extent, forced to follow mainstream fashion so as not to look out of date, Adrian nevertheless introduced interesting interpretations of these fashions, added innovative details and at times introduced original items that successfully crossed over. The Eugenie hat he created for *Romance* (1930) was widely copied and set the tone for the decade's millinery fashions; equally, his *Letty Lynton* dress (1932) spawned thousands of copies and contributed to the fashion for big, ruffled sleeves. However, his most important contribution was his role in popularising the accentuated shoulder (through shoulder pads and/or sculpted detailing), which dominated the decade's silhouette and which he developed specifically for Joan Crawford to (in his own words) 'balance out her figure'.

In 1942, after leaving MGM, Adrian established his own fashion house. The Beverly Hills establishment attracted considerable attention from both private and commercial clients and his collections were widely promoted by the press. During the war years Adrian contributed to the development of a home-grown American design industry that developed silhouettes and fashions independently of Paris. His signature silhouette of broad shoulders combined with a narrow skirt dominated American fashion until the advent of the New Look.

Opposite *Adrian with some of his costume sketches. During the period he was contracted to MGM studios (1928–42), Adrian defined the look of some of Hollywood's leading lights, including Joan Crawford, Jean Harlow and Greta Garbo.*

Left *Joan Crawford, appearing in the title role of Clarence Brown's 1932 film, Letty Lynton. This dress is often referred to as 'the other Letty Lynton gown'. In truth the entire film's wardrobe is a tour de fashion force and showed Adrian's talent in not only translating fashion into costume but moving it forward through his costume designs. This dress was famously copied by Roberto Cavalli for Autumn 2005.*

Accentuated Shoulders

The late Twenties and early Thirties witnessed the introduction of a new silhouette and fashions that once again emphasised certain areas of the body, rather than simply hanging alongside it. With the reintroduction of the waist in garments of this decade, the shoulders equally became accentuated.

The introduction of these harder or moulded shoulders is often credited to Schiaparelli, and there is enough evidence to suggest that she was one of the first, if not the first, to present this more defined shape in Haute Couture. However, we need to look towards Hollywood to get a more complete picture.

Costume designer Adrian created for Joan Crawford throughout the decade. According to his own account, he started introducing all manner of sleeves and shoulder pads into Crawford's costumes to balance out her hips. It must be remembered that Hollywood stars were veritable fashion icons and that their looks were widely copied by women worldwide. Adrian's ruffled *Letty Lynton* dress (1932) became so popular that department stores could not keep up with the demand for copies, and magazines on both sides of the Atlantic featured dress patterns for adults' and children's versions. Crawford was arguably one of the greatest actresses of the decade, so what she wore on and off screen undoubtedly impacted upon fashion as a whole.

Although the vast majority of Haute Couture designers denounced Hollywood as vulgar, they could hardly deny or ignore its importance, and most couturiers quickly introduced garments with more accentuated shoulders. Lucien Lelong hit the nail on the head when he declared about the Hollywood/Paris relationship: 'We corroborate each other's instinct.'

——— Broad-shouldered tailored jackets, puffed, butterfly and banjo sleeves and the use of dress clips all served to draw attention to the upper body.

⊕ The accentuated shoulder, like the bias cut, was a clear silver-screen favourite. Early examples include the leg-of-mutton sleeves designed by Walter Plunkett for Irene Dunne in *Cimarron* (1931).

⊕ Accentuated shoulders remained popular throughout the decade, but by 1937 they took on a less frivolous and much more masculine feel, possibly reflecting the political shifts in Europe and the build-up to war. It was only in 1947, with the introduction of the New Look, that shoulders lost their hard edge.

Fur

Although the world economy was plunged into a depression for much of the decade, in the realms of high fashion luxury and opulence were still the order of the day. While dresses became less heavily decorated than those of the Twenties (the vogue for beading and embroidery had waned by 1928), fabrics and accessories were made from high-quality materials and thus luxury shifted from the decoration to the fabric and cut.

Fur trims had been popular in the Twenties, but the Thirties did not just stick to trims: fur was in abundance and the rarer and more exotic the pelt, the more desirable and glamorous. Silver-fox opera coats, sealskin capelets, monkey-fur boleros, leopard cloaks… it seemed every animal under the sun could be turned into fashion.

This fashion was also heavily promoted by Hollywood designers, who used it to excess for the costumes of their leading ladies. Promotional shots of the greats of the day such as Jean Harlow, Marlene Dietrich, Claudette Colbert, Joan Crawford, Carole Lombard and Ginger Rogers unfailingly showed the actresses dressed in luxurious gowns and enveloped in the most sumptuous fur coats, shrugs and stoles. The accessible nature of cinema, combined with the aggressive Hollywood marketing machine, meant that these women influenced fashion and could sell garments, which is why so many of them were signed up to lucrative endorsement contracts. This led ordinary women to aspire to their lives and styles, and companies, including ready-to-wear companies, heavily exploited this. Sears' catalogue had actresses 'design' special collections for them, and indeed their womenswear range included many styles popularised by Hollywood, including fur.

⊕ In Paris, Schiaparelli, Lanvin, Molyneux, Maggy Rouff and Mainbocher all offered innovative fur creations, often combining two or more different pelts.

While exotic pelts were reserved for the elite only, ready-to-wear companies offered cheap pelts such as muskrat, marmot and lamb; rabbit fur was dyed to resemble nearly anything but what it actually was.

⊕ For those who couldn't afford even inferior fur pelts there was American broadtail, or 'processed lamb' as Sears advertised it, and a wide variety of cotton-pile faux furs.

The Bias Cut

'Bias cut' refers to cutting a fabric diagonally instead of along the cross- or the straight grain. This technique allows designers to use the greater elasticity and stretch in the diagonal direction of the cloth, which facilitates draping and results in fabric clinging closely to the body. Bias cutting was employed in the Middle Ages when it was used to make hose fit more closely, but after the invention of knitting (which creates an elasticated structure) it was not used to create whole garments until the twentieth century.

The couturière credited with the 1930s shift to bias cutting is Madeleine Vionnet, who is affectionately known as 'queen of the bias cut'. Vionnet trained at Callot Sœurs, where she was introduced to the technique. She had a keen interest in the natural female shape and, consequently, in ancient Greek costume. Like Chanel and Patou, she wanted to develop a more natural female dress shape, but unlike the former two who focused on material, Vionnet put the emphasis on technique: bias cutting and draping hugged the body but did not distort it.

These clinging dresses with minimal ornamentation received an unexpected boost from Hollywood, which dressed its leading ladies in glamorous Vionnet-inspired evening robes – the best example being Jean Harlow in the 1933 film *Dinner at Eight* (see page 84).

However great their on-screen popularity, floor-length bias-cut dresses became mostly obsolete after the outbreak of World War Two, as they were considered wasteful and therefore unpatriotic.

— Silent screen goddess and original It Girl Clara Bow in a metallic bias-cut lamé dress, 1931. The dress is a clear derivative of a Vionnet model, but in the Thirties it was Hollywood, not Paris, that became the main communicator of popular fashion styles owing to its democratic nature.

⊕ In the late Twenties, after the dramatic fall of hemlines and the emergence of a more fitted silhouette, Madeleine Vionnet started creating floor-length bias-cut gowns in luxurious pale silks and silver and gold lamé, often featuring halter necks and/or exposed backs.

⊕ The liquid line created by the bias cut could be exaggerated to such an extent that a woman could appear to be nearly naked while being fully clothed.

◑ Vionnet's fashion innovations served Hollywood in several ways. The minimal ornamentation (such as the lack of beading or embroidery) meant the dress was not only silent (a crucial consideration in the Thirties 'talkies') but it would show up well on screen.

1940s

The Forties can roughly be divided into two equal halves: the first a period of unprecedented worldwide conflict, the second a return to normality.

Relatively little has been written on fashion during World War Two – this is because, to many, it seems almost disrespectful in retrospect to think (let alone talk) about fashion at a time when millions were suffering and dying. However, by ignoring fashion during this period we have encouraged the myth that during times of intense crisis fashion simply stops and becomes unimportant.

In reality, nothing could be further from the truth. Fashion production was vitally important to keep economies afloat, and the flexible nature of the garment industry caused it to be involved in, and often redirected towards, the production of military uniforms and kit. Another reason why so little is written about war fashions is to be found in our original definition of the word set out in the Introduction. Fashion is about cyclical change, but at a time of material shortages, austerity regulations and rationing, change naturally ground almost to a halt and was only to be found, in many cases, in the details. Furthermore, owing to women's increasingly active engagement in work and public life as they took over men's jobs, clothing had to be practical before anything else, and unlike in previous decades practical *meant* practical, not just comfortable.

Braced for Conflict

Germany's invasion of Poland on 1 September 1939 came as no great surprise, and many European countries had been quietly preparing for the inevitability of war for several years. Only a few days prior to the invasions, the Parisian Haute Couture collections had been shown to noticeably fewer international customers than usual, proof that tension was in the air. The collections had also captured that feeling: daywear was characterised by increasing practicality (albeit luxurious practicality), tweed and wool suits, boxy, masculine shoulders and narrowly tailored waists; only evening wear still had its head in the clouds and favoured full-skirted dresses with sweetheart necklines, matched with trimmed boleros.

The collection directly after the declaration of war wholly reflected the reality of conflict, and warm and versatile fashions were the order of the day. Swiss-born designer Robert Piguet showed a reversible wool 'air-raid' outfit, the cape of which doubled as a blanket. Schiaparelli presented a one-piece zippered jumpsuit available in petrol blue and her trademark shocking pink, as well as coats with deep 'kangaroo' pockets so one could hurriedly stash essentials in them in case of an air raid. British designer Edward Henry Molyneux suggested chic pyjamas suitable for home and shelter wear, and Lanvin showed practical day dresses. Knitwear, hooded jersey dresses and an abundance of fur featured in many collections; even evening wear morphed into pragmatic luxury, presenting long-sleeved evening gowns and jackets to keep the night cold out in case of unexpected visits to the bomb shelter. This design realism was joined by a good degree of patriotism and militarism: colours such as 'aeroplane grey' and 'French soil beige' were used in military-style jackets, and scarves printed with French regimental flags were *en vogue*.

Above *Wartime news photograph captioned 'the very latest fashion in air-raid shelter wear is a slip-on dressing gown....' Throughout the war several garments were developed for civilians in response to their new daily reality, the siren suit (right), named after the siren that alerted civilians to imminent air raids, was one such item. The marrying of necessity with fashion (even if frequently it was only in name) disproves the commonly held assumption that an interest in fashion stops during times of conflict, whereas in fact it was a means of maintaining a modicum of normality.*

Practicality, expressed both through silhouette and fabric choices in this first wartime collection, was to become the defining feature of fashion both in Paris and abroad. Not only was this common sense, in most countries directly or indirectly affected by the war, sparseness and abandonment of luxury was part of a national discourse of patriotism, survival and victory, and indeed became a powerful propaganda tool.

Fashion Under Occupation

When German troops entered Paris on 14 June 1940, in their immaculately tailored Hugo Boss uniforms (Boss had been a member of the Nazi Party since 1931 and supplied uniforms for the Hitler Youth and the SS), the city resembled a ghost town. The government and many civilians had fled; those who remained, including the couture salons, had closed their businesses and fastened their shutters. Within days, however, businesses started to reopen and in August, when the Nazi authorities decreed that any closed businesses would be confiscated, more salons followed.

Facing inevitable military defeat, France had signed an armistice that saw the country cut in two, with the Northern Zone, including Paris, under German occupation. To add insult to injury, France had to pay extortionate occupation costs at unfavourable exchange rates, which plunged the country into economic turmoil. Borders were closed, no one was allowed in or out, and crossing from the occupied Northern Zone into the Southern Zone or vice versa was exceptionally difficult. Furthermore, France was faced with millions of displaced people. So, with the country in political, financial and social turmoil, combined with a lack of communication, the rest of the world reasonably assumed that Paris had ceased its fashion operations.

However, contrary to popular belief then and now, the majority of the Haute Couture trade remained open for the duration of the war, a fact that many surviving salons or brands do not always like to acknowledge as it inevitably raises some uncomfortable questions.

At the outset of the occupation, Molyneux, Creed and Mainbocher had shut up shop and subsequently remained closed, as their owners had fled the country. Lucien Lelong, head of the Chambre Syndicale, became increasingly worried about the closures as so many people's livelihoods depended on the Haute Couture industry. He decided that it was his duty to keep the

Left *Adolf Hitler in Hugo Boss uniform visiting Paris after the city's fall and occupation by the German army, 1940.*

La Collection des Permissionnaires

By the spring of 1940, practicality went up a further notch as hemlines were raised, resulting in shorter skirts and dresses that were ideal for cycling. Separates became increasingly prevalent to increase garments' use, and durable fabric choices were nearly universal. This spring collection would become known as *La Collection des Permissionnaires*, named after the special permission or dispensation passes granted to male couturiers who had been called up for service but were granted leave to come home and finish their collections. This indicates just how culturally and financially important France considered its Haute Couture industry.

Left *A Parisian woman during the Occupation wearing a practical but stylish ensemble (possibly couture) is evidence that even in times of hardship style was not compromised for those who could afford it.*

salons running, which he would later describe as a sign of defiance to the occupier. The rest of the world was less than impressed with this reasoning. Their objections centred on the continued production and consumption of luxury goods at a time when the rest of France and indeed the rest of the world was living with severe rationing, suffering austerity measures and acute shortages of essentials.

Preserving Parisian Couture

Throughout the war Hitler was adamant that the couture industry should be moved to Berlin and Vienna so he could fulfil his dream of making these two cities the fashion capitals of the new world he envisioned (and to humiliate the French). Lucien Lelong fought the move and repeatedly met with the German authorities

to ensure the industry's survival, but also to request special dispensation for couturiers to have access to luxury fabrics, pelts and trimmings. Again, these meetings and 'favours' would show Haute Couture in a very negative light after the war.

While countries such as Britain and the United States saw few changes to fashion during the war in terms of silhouette – both because of shortages or rationing and because neither had a home-grown design industry, having merely followed what Paris was doing – Parisian Haute Couture evolved as if it really were business as usual. In the four years of the occupation, waists grew smaller, hips larger, and drapery was common. The nineteenth-century influence that had been creeping into fashion in the closing years of the Thirties became explicit through bustled and fuller skirts. Hats grew to

enormous proportions and skirted the boundaries of good taste. It was the hats that particularly offended the first journalists to reach a liberated Paris in 1944. The foreign press could not believe their eyes when they saw Parisian women in full skirts and embroidered jackets, given that other nations' silhouettes had remained rather tight-fitting and short throughout the war, in line with austerity regulations that forbade any decoration that had no functional purpose.

Even more shocking was their realisation that nearly a hundred Haute Couture salons and luxury businesses had remained open. This news was considered so problematic and inflammatory that US officials tried to impose a press embargo to prevent it reaching international audiences. The news did get out, and the rest of the world responded with disbelief, disgust and outrage, understandably enough in the circumstances of the time.

Though it is easy to make a blanket judgement of collaboration, life (and even fashion) is never that simple. While on the one hand Lelong's insistent efforts to keep the industry open in difficult times can be seen as selfish collaboration, on the other hand it needs to be remembered that his actions saved thousands of workers from forced labour in Germany and kept thousands of families fed.

Opposite Christian Dior in his atelier, 1947. The dressmaker's dummies show the undergarments required to achieve the New Look silhouette; in the background is a petticoat and (centre) a corset with built-in mini-crini/ paniers. The stockings, dainty hat, muff, hat pins and jewellery are the accessories needed to complete the ultra-ladylike style and are evidence of a commitment to consumption to achieve it.

Dior and the New Look

In 1945, the international press mostly shunned the first free collections; those who did attend condemned them. In reaction to its perceived transgressions, Paris attempted to appease the foreign press and buyers by toning down the extravagance, so as to fall in line with the understated fashions in New York and London – a move also designed to ensure Parisian design could be legally sold in countries still operating rationing – but to little avail. By the autumn of the next year Parisian couture was on the brink of bankruptcy.

As early as 1944, American *Vogue* had tried to defuse the situation by offering Lelong a platform to explain himself. He stated that he and other couturiers had no idea of the austerity measures and rationing programmes operating in other war-stricken countries, and so tried to justify Paris's continued extravagance.

In a bold move, several American journalists decided that the only way to help Paris survive was by giving the 1947 collections positive reviews and focusing on the clothes rather than the context. This positive attitude was facilitated by the arrival of a new couturier: Christian Dior.

Dior had trained at Lelong and his talent had attracted the eye of France's richest man: the textile industrialist Marcel Boussac. Having made cloth for German uniforms during the war, Boussac was forced to 'diversify' his business and associate himself with less problematic activities fast. The agreement was that Boussac would bankroll Dior's maison in exchange for the designer's commitment to creating garments that used an extravagant amount of fabric to increase Boussac's sales. The result of this agreement was the Corolle line, a silhouette comprising a full calf-length skirt worn with voluminous petticoats or crinolines, a wasp waist and rounded shoulders. The press gushed over this bold return to luxury and excess, which was indeed appealing to many after years of making do. To international audiences the silhouette was so novel and represented such a break with the recent past that the press christened it the New Look.

The reality, of course, was that inside France this look was anything but new, and a mere evolution rather than a break, as this variation on a mid-nineteenth-century silhouette had been developing since 1939. In fact, several couture collections had featured similar evening-wear silhouettes in 1945 and 1946, but it was Dior who transformed this glamorous evening elegance into luxurious daywear.

Dior's return to a perfect hourglass figure was achieved through corsetry and crinolines, and while the press piled on the praise, not everyone was enamoured. Both in the UK and the USA, politicians and women's groups alike condemned the new style for its conspicuous luxury and outdated, regressive femininity, which once again saw women hiding their legs and shackled in structured undergarments.

While the elite was quick to adopt it as an overt marker of status (but also as an embracement of a post-war return to normality, luxury and peace), the mass market took somewhat longer to convince. However, by 1948 ready-to-wear companies were featuring fuller skirts in their catalogues and women's magazines ran features on how to insert extra panels into skirts to achieve this fuller silhouette. Dior's star was rising and would remain high for most of the decade ahead.

Opposite *Wool melton day dress by Dior, c. 1947. The typical soft Dior shoulders are accentuated by a capelet collar.*

Right *This wartime Haute Couture outfit shows that the post-war appearance of the New Look silhouette was in fact the outcome of a silhouette change that had been steadily developing for several years. The wider skirts and closely accentuated waist of this ensemble clearly hints at things to come.*

Madame Grès

Above *Bodice detail of a Grès dress showing the exquisite craftsmanship of the painstakingly pleated fabric. The natural fluidity and seemingly relaxed nature of Grès's silhouettes often belied the vast amounts of time and fabric that went into their creation.*

Germaine Emilie Krebs, known in fashion as Alix Barton or simply Alix, opened her first salon – Maison Alix – in 1932. The following year the name was changed to Alix Barton, combining Germaine and her co-worker Juliette Barton's surnames; however, by 1934 the 'Barton' was dropped and the house continued to be known as Alix until 1942, when it was rechristened Maison Grès.

Madame Grès was most known for her draped Grecian-style goddess gowns in silk, taffeta and jersey, whose clean and minimal appearance belied their intricate construction techniques. Like Vionnet's before her, Grès's silhouettes were meant to complement the female body, not reshape it.

Grès had studied painting and sculpting before shifting her endeavours to fashion, and her background in fine art was always present in her design and technique. After briefly working in millinery she trained at Maison Premet, a house known for its attention to detail and perfect fit. This training in perfection combined with her extensive knowledge of classical sculpture led to the development of Grès's signature style: the draped dress.

Her Greco-Roman creations were painstakingly draped and pleated using excessive lengths of fabric (14–26 yards, 13–24 metres); a dress could take several hundred hours to make, as each pleat was hand-draped; Grès literally sculpted her fabric forms. To this end she used live mannequins, designing and constructing garments directly onto their bodies. The draperies of her gowns were testament to her technical virtuosity: swags of continuous strips of fabric were incorporated into the front and back of each gown, giving them a sense of classical sculpture. Her signature technique earned her the titles Sphinx of Fashion and Queen of Drapery. Aside from classical sculpture her influences included togas, capes and wraps, in addition to wider Asian and Eastern cultural influences, which she translated in a clean and modern way into fashion.

The house remained open during World War Two; however, Grès's liberal use of fabric to create her hand-sewn pleats broke the strict German allowances on fabric yardage and on several occasions the house was temporarily shut down. Post-war she experimented with simpler cuts and less draping (to reduce the yardage so that the garments could be legally exported) but continued to look towards traditional Asian dress for inspiration. In the Fifties she introduced cut-out dresses, featuring little 'windows' that revealed the back or a shoulder. While she continued to focus largely on exclusive Haute Couture for the remainder of her career, Madame Grès's influence on fashion has been extensive and contemporary designers still regularly cite her as their inspiration.

Left *Madame Grès continued
to design until the Eighties
when, well into her eighties
herself, she finally retired.*

Charles James

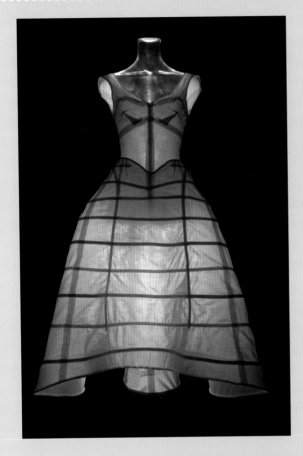

on both sides of the Atlantic was taking notice of this young man with a gift for lavish sculptural clothing.

From New York, James moved to London where he opened a store in Mayfair, attracting the *crème* of London society, and a Parisian establishment soon followed. James treated his dresses as works of art – as did his customers – and they were priced accordingly. Although largely self-taught, his mastery of cutting and tailoring combined with his idiosyncratic vision led to many innovative and unexpected methods, including off-grain cuts, displaced seams, asymmetric draping that eliminated darts, quilting and spiral cutting.

He developed garments with adjustable fit, which meant that two sizes could accommodate most body shapes, and built-in design features such as the 'Pavlovian' waistband that could expand after a meal. These innovations and his cutting techniques showed an advanced anatomical understanding of and fascination with the female body – but unlike Vionnet or Grès, his fixation came from his belief that the feminine figure was 'intrinsically wrong' and thus had to be corrected through tailoring.

This belief saw James continually trying to perfect his creations, but also reworking and reusing designs and patterns from previous seasons. This gave him a library of interchangeable dress elements that could be endlessly combined into the perfect creation. The obsession with perfection that made James a well-respected innovator also proved to be his downfall, as the cost and waiting time for one of his garments proved too much for his clients and the hours spent on perfecting creations meant the cost of labour could never be recouped. James retired in 1958. Although he is now best remembered for his sculpted ball gowns (most famously, his cloverleaf gown), his capes, his down-quilted puffer jacket (much admired by Salvador Dalí), coats and spiral dresses (named 'taxi dresses' as they were so simple to take off, it could be done in the back of a taxi), he also introduced fashion to thoroughly new ideas and shapes. Dior even credited James with influencing his 1947 New Look.

Charles James was an Anglo-American designer whose avant-garde creations are credited with transforming fashion design from the Twenties until the end of his career in the late Fifties.

In 1926, at the age of 19, James opened a hat shop in Chicago, to the great dismay of his army officer father. His mother's connections saw him patronised by Chicago society ladies, and his charm and flair for design gained him loyal followers. His design ethos and the method for which he would become known in his dressmaking were already present: James shaped his hats directly on his clients' heads by cutting, twisting, pinning and scrunching felt or straw into whimsical shapes. After two years he moved his business to New York and added dresses to his output. His friend, the socialite, designer and photographer Cecil Beaton, promoted his work in *Vogue* and soon the fashion press

Opposite *Structured undergarments for a Charles James gown. The one-piece petticoat slip evidences the similarity of his creations with 1850s crinoline cages.*

Left *Two Charles James silhouettes that demonstrate his creative pattern cutting and his hallmark interplay between voluminous skirts and tight-fitting bodices.*

Christian Dior

Christian Dior briefly ran a contemporary art gallery before becoming involved in fashion design. In 1937 he was employed by couturier Robert Piguet, who taught Dior the virtues of simplicity and elegance. While at Piguet, Dior designed several collections, all of which included well-received silhouettes. Dior left Maison Piguet when he was called up for military service at the outbreak of war, and only returned to fashion in 1942.

In that year he joined Maison Lucien Lelong, where he worked alongside Pierre Balmain. In December 1946, with the financial backing of Marcel Boussac, a fabric magnate, he founded his own house and only a few months later presented his Corolle (circlet of flower petals) line, which was rechristened the 'New Look' by Carmel Snow, editor-in-chief of *Harper's Bazaar*.

To anyone who had not spent the war in Paris (where a more voluptuous rounded line and historicist influences had been developing since 1939), his designs appeared extremely novel and they came to be seen as a rejection of austerity. The controversy generated by the look saw Dior elevated almost overnight to the most famous designer in the world. While the flower silhouette remained a popular choice throughout the Fifties, it was far from being Dior's only contribution to design – each season he played with skirt widths (from the padded to the fitted), necklines and coat shapes.

However, he stayed true to the more mature, elegant (and, to many young women, outdated) femininity he had introduced in 1947. He repeatedly used hip padding, corsetry, boning, petticoats and his favoured wasp waist, to create his ideal curvaceous hourglass silhouette.

Dior was an astute businessman and capitalised on the press furore generated by the New Look by launching a ready-to-wear boutique in New York, a perfume aimed specifically at the American market, and – most importantly – by signing a very lucrative licensing deal with a US hosiery company, for the rights to manufacture Dior stockings.

His business acumen was also present in the marketing of his own couture collection; knowing his clients were wealthy, rather conservative and did not always have model bodies, he hired mannequins in different shapes and sizes to highlight how his creations would look on different women. His clientele and his own design vision meant that after the New Look, Dior cannot be described as a great innovator. Instead, he preferred to adhere to a tried and tested economic model in which a third of his collection were new silhouettes, a third adaptations of previous successes and a third proven classic pieces. He died while on holiday in 1957; the house of Dior remains synonymous with classic elegance even today.

Left *Dior's fashions, and several of his contemporaries', were sold to the public as a return to normality and pre-war luxury – a material manifestation that the worst was over. However, Dior's opulence and excessive fabric use was in part influenced by pressure from his backer. Textile production and consumption had plummeted during the war and to revive the industry Haute Couture designers were encouraged to be wasteful in their creations.*

La Petite Robe

La petite robe ('the little dress') was a staple throughout World War Two and remained popular with many women when the conflict ended. The narrow-waisted, knee-length dress with accentuated shoulders had been popular daywear in the late Thirties, but became invaluable in the first half of the Forties. Clothing shortages, rationing and austerity measures had a profound impact on design at this time, and the need to save fabric ensured that hemlines remained raised. These shorter dresses were also infinitely practical for walking and for war work (for which unmarried young women were enlisted). In each European country affected by the conflict (and in the United States), this style of dress can be found in fashion publications of the time. However, to attribute its popularity merely to practicality misses the point, as the *petite robe* was a staple in the wartime Haute Couture collections too.

In the closing years of the war, the couture versions of the dress steadily acquired more ample skirts, hinting at a development towards the New Look. After the conflict this style of dress remained popular particularly in Britain – where rationing continued into the Fifties – and in the United States, where elegant versions by American designers were favoured by many over the New Look silhouette with its lower hemline and cumbersome skirts.

—— Simple belted dresses (right) were a fashion staple in the majority of countries affected by conflict. The fashion was a response to a greater need for comfort and often severe rationing. Its shape changed little throughout the war and thus made the *petite robe* a durable staple.

⊕ In Haute Couture circles, Paquin and Lanvin presented their versions of the *petite robe* with embroidered military-style jackets, while Nina Ricci suggested hers with a fur box coat – yet the basic shape of the dress was nearly identical.

⊕ In summer the dress came in cotton or linen, in winter in wool or crepe. While couture versions often featured embroidery, less elitist versions tended to be plainer, although small floral patterns and polka dots were also popular. These smaller textile designs added some colour and cheer to the average woman's wardrobe and became a popular choice for both ready-to-wear and home dressmakers as the small pattern repeat ensured very little fabric wastage.

Tailored gingham jacket and skirt ensemble with matching accessories. Although luxury fabrics were unavailable, style was not compromised by those who could afford it. Wedge shoes, gloves and sometimes ostentatious hats were hallmarks of Parisian fashion during World War Two and the latter attracted much negative attention upon liberation.

⊕ All-in-one 'siren suits' for ordinary women were first and foremost practical. However, Paris presented versions that married practicality with high fashion: Piguet and Schiaparelli offered luxury tailored versions with built-in capes that doubled up as blankets.

⊕ Some couturiers made elegant cycling outfits in durable wools. Warm pyjamas (sometimes trimmed and lined with fur) and matching housecoats became a staple in response to fuel shortages, and evening dresses came with matching capes that could be thrown on in the event of an air raid.

Practical Chic

Practical chic can mean a variety of things in the context of 1940s fashion. During the war it refers to the changes made to garments out of necessity (shorter hemlines due to rationing and the need for greater mobility, separates to make clothes more versatile in an era of scarcity), by law (many countries had strict guidelines on how much fabric and elastic, how many zippers and buttons a garment was allowed to use) and out of common sense.

In addition, it can also refer to the 'new' type of outfits and garments that appeared in response to the extreme conditions. Siren suits – all-in-one jumpsuit-style outfits intended to be put on in haste and made from warm fabric to keep the wearer comfortable during nights in the air-raid shelter – are a perfect example of this.

These changes that came about out of necessity would have a lasting impact, in particular on American fashion. America, like many other nations, introduced rationing (1941) and, due to Paris's isolation, actively encouraged homegrown design. Claire McCardell and Hattie Carnegie had started designing in previous decades, and during the war became household names. The fashions they proposed were a mixture of smart-casual daywear consisting of lots of separates inspired by the campus look, and stylish evening wear influenced by luxurious floor-length Hollywood gowns. Their sportswear was affordable, comfortable and stylish and became known as the American Look, which reaped great success in the following decade with young women who valued elegance but found the Parisian notion of elegance too restraining both physically and financially.

The New Look

In 1947 the newly established Parisian Haute Couture house Dior presented a collection that grabbed the attention of the fashion press and women worldwide. In Britain the fashion was immediately condemned by the Labour government as silly and wasteful, while in Dallas the Little Below the Knee Club was established as a protest against what its members considered a regressive fashion that forced women's legs into hiding once more. In Paris, models wearing the latest fashions were attacked during an outdoor photoshoot by angry citizens protesting against this blatant elitism, while so many still lived in dire straits.

Regardless of the press attention, the New Look silhouette was not an immediate and universal success. While the remaining (although heavily reduced) number of couture buyers indulged, when it came to a mass audience the trickle-down effect took much longer than is often realised. This was partly due to the aforementioned disgust at such extravagance at a time of war, but equally because ready-to-wear manufacturers realised they would struggle to offer the fashion at a reasonable price. They would either have to raise their prices (a complete impossibility in a post-war economy) or reduce their profit (an equally ludicrous proposition).

Thus, while the New Look was perhaps not the veritable design revolution it is remembered as, its true value, arguably one far greater than fashion, was that it constituted a material response to economic problems and hence became a symbol of a specific time and place.

The New Look was one dominated by wasp waists, soft, rounded shoulders and vast skirts (achieved through the use of ruffled underskirts) topped off with tiny hats secured under the chin with delicate veils.

Dior's return to the perfect hourglass figure was achieved through corsetry, crinoline-like skirts and lower hemlines. The most famous of the Corolle-line silhouettes, this image has become symbolic of the New Look as it highlights all its key characteristics: rounded soft shoulders, a nipped (corseted) waist, and a midi skirt with petticoats.

⊕ Although slow to catch on, by early 1948 leisurewear in America began to take its cues from Dior, though the style was adjusted to be more comfortable by lowering the hemlines from wartime lengths and removing the boning from dresses. Around the same time, Sears' catalogue offered New Look-inspired skirts, dresses and suits and women's magazines across the globe instructed their readers on how to adapt clothes to the longer hemline lengths by dropping the yokes on skirts and even knitting extra bands that could be inserted at regular intervals.

1950s

The Fifties were a decade of change and contradiction: global economies boomed but the return to peace in the previous decade – and its accompanying optimism and assumption that it was once again 'business as usual' – was all too quickly tainted by the start of the Korean war, the increasing divide between the West and the USSR, and the anti-colonial uprisings that were sweeping the Third World. By the end of the decade, the political and social movements that would change the world had taken root and the post-war 'normality' was a pipe dream. It could be argued that this was the decade in which past and future battled it out, and this battle characterised all spheres of life, including fashion.

Dior's New Look had taken the fashion world by storm in the closing years of the Forties and signalled a return to luxury after years of austerity. His vision of luxury, though called 'new', was in many ways a throwback to the 1850s: his nipped waists, rounded shoulders, padded skirts and lowered hemlines all echoed mid-nineteenth-century fashionable attire, albeit with a modern twist. However, contrary to what many historians have tried to argue, the post-war years were not some sinister conspiracy to get women back into the kitchen – and neither were Dior's ensembles a weapon in some battle of the sexes. The New Look (and the many other romantic fashions around in the early years of the Fifties) said more about the human desire for luxury and normality than it did about gender divides.

New Romantics

Dior's vision of how the female form should be adorned changed from season to season and he proposed a variety of silhouettes. His Zig Zag designs utilised asymmetrical draping to hug curves (a look that was championed throughout the Fifties by Jacques Fath, whose elegant, sexy and glamorous creations were highly coveted). His trompe-l'œil designs used floating panels to give a sense of movement to highly tailored ensembles. His Princess and Tulip lines offered further

Above *Models from the Maison Dior with Marc Bohan at Paris airport in 1955, en route to Washington to present the Winter collection at the French Embassy.*

distinctive silhouettes. The H-line featured a pushed-up bust and a Tudor-style bodice, while the A-line was characterised by its narrow shoulders, high bust and wide flaring skirts. The latter evolved into his later Y-line, which retained its emphasis on the bust but replaced the wider skirts with ones that narrowly followed the contours of the body as if it were a flower stem.

But, throughout these changes, all Dior's creations remained true to his central design tenet: that a dress should hug, mould and enhance the female shape, or, as he put it, 'save women from nature'.

Other promoters of this design ethos were French designers Jacques Fath and Pierre Balmain, who were particularly known for their romantic and extravagant cocktail dresses and formal evening wear. British-born Charles James, America's first couturier, often followed the Dior line in terms of waist and hem placement; however, his highly structured aesthetic gave a less romantic and far more abstract and modern feel to his creations.

Balenciaga the Sculptor

One designer who rejected this 'classic' treatment of the female body (and, from the outset of the decade, offered alternatives) was the Spanish couturier Cristóbal Balenciaga. Where Dior's approach was romantic, Balenciaga's was sculptural; instead of contouring the body, he 'built' clothing around it like architecture, by playing around with volume and proportion through cut and draping. With their intricate and exaggerated shoulders, sleeves and collars, his designs were not universally popular – they were in many ways decades ahead of their time – yet Balenciaga had a small and devout group of followers that would grow as the decade wore on. His silhouette changes were much slower than Dior's, as he focused more on the art and craft of dressmaking than on chasing the next headline. A master of proportions, his approach both in ethos and execution would have a fundamental impact on the 'alternative' Japanese and Belgian designers of the Eighties and Nineties, exemplifying just how visionary his designs were. Like Vionnet before him, Balenciaga was a sculptor of fabric and, together with Madame Grès and Givenchy, his approach was truly forward-looking, offering an alternative to the figure-enhancing designs of the Dior camp.

Couture à la Coco

Chanel rejected the aesthetics of both Dior and Balenciaga, challenging the post-war dominance of male couturiers. After an extended stay in Switzerland, prompted by her wartime involvement with a Nazi officer and subsequent questioning by the Free French Forces, she returned to the fashion scene in 1954.

Unlike her contemporary male counterparts, she established herself as the friend of women and a role model for them: her Fifties designs, like her earlier work, adhered to an ethos that foregrounded elegant comfort for the modern lady. Chanel despised the way the Dior camp had once again shackled women by reintroducing corsetry and stiff tailoring, and she deplored Balenciaga and his followers for their

Opposite *Balenciaga coat, Autumn/Winter 1957. This coat is one of several from his 1957 collection that feature oversized but perfectly proportioned collars. His preference for monochrome creations with minimal embellishment foregrounds his innovative pattern cutting.*

Above *Chanel in her apartments at the Ritz Hotel, Paris, wearing one of her collarless Chanel suits.*

treatment of the female body as a canvas on which to hang their creations. Instead, she promoted an updated version of her jersey Chanel suit. Its Fifties incarnation was a wool-tweed combination suit, consisting of a hip-length tailored jacket and a straight knee-length skirt – elegant, understated and comfortable. The collarless jacket was meant to be worn open, and hence the blouse became a major fashion feature.

Above *Swedish model Lisa Fonssagrives in a tailored suit featuring a long pencil skirt and a fitted jacket with a peplum, as featured in* Harper's Bazaar, *1951.*

Chanel was not the only one to elevate this item to a veritable fashion staple – many couturiers played around with sleeves and trimmings to create the ultimate blouse, realising the importance it held in the modern working woman's wardrobe. Designs ranged from the elegantly functional to the dainty and decorative. Givenchy's 1952 Bettina blouse, made of shirting with a wide-open upright neck and full, ruffled broderie anglaise sleeves, became an instant success that spawned innumerable copies despite its less than functional nature.

Day and Night

While it is easy to focus exclusively on the exquisite and luxurious evening gowns of the Fifties as so many fashion histories do, it is important to remember that all couturiers also offered daywear looks which were far less over-the-top and restrictive. Pencil or trumpet skirts were teamed with twinsets, fitted sweaters or blouses over which boleros and jackets of varying lengths and cuts were worn. Collars came in all styles and the colour palette of the decade was varied and rich, often drawing inspiration from Asia: sapphire and peacock blues and emerald greens joined other favourites such as orange, apricot, lavender, purple, pinks, browns and of course the most elegant colour of all, black.

These different and at times seemingly conflicting fashion design developments of the Fifties were in fact not so much a symptom of disagreement but of a widening of choice in terms of fashionable attire and looks, depending on the client's preference. Equally, different looks and garments were worn at different times of the day as post-war polite society witnessed a near-Victorian return to etiquette rules about correct behaviour and good taste which dictated the appropriateness of garments, fabrics and accessories based on occasion and place. So a Chanel tweed suit was appropriate for afternoon city excursions but would be considered too underdressed for a formal evening dinner or ball at which a Dior, Balenciaga, Fath or James ball gown would be expected. Even Chanel was not immune from this highly regimented sartorial order and proposed more formal tight-fitting evening dresses that many women found almost impossible to sit down in. Cocktail dresses were worn for less formal evening occasions and again all couturiers offered their version.

Couture Goes Mainstream

That is not to say that Haute Couture did not undergo major reform during the decade. Having suffered a significant blow in the immediate post-war years, from 1947 onwards Haute Couture re-established its reign as fashion leader; however, the mode of its importance and impact changed significantly.

In the Fifties, couture was increasingly selling to the mass market via the wholesale industry; private clients had seriously dwindled during World War Two and had never quite reattained their pre-war numbers. Wholesale buyers (mostly American) could either pay to view the collections from which to get their design inspiration, rent 'bonded models' for a certain time period or buy *toiles* (finished designs executed in calico) or actual Haute Couture gowns and copy them. Their choice depended on what market they were supplying, and thus what level of accuracy and detail was needed.

The American Look

As Paris had been cut off from the rest of the world for four years during the war, New York, like so many other places, was initially confused as to what to do about fashion design, having been so heavily reliant on direction from Paris. Soon, however, a distinctive New York look – sportswear that married elegance with comfort – was being pioneered by the likes of Claire McCardell. It became known as the American Look and its casual-chic character still underpins New York Fashion Week collections today. This American Look was particularly popular with younger women who applauded its style, comfort, easy materials and designs (which, unlike Parisian collections, included pedal-pusher trousers and Bermuda shorts), its often higher-than-Dior hemline, and more 'democratic' prices; and so it became yet another option in the widening lexicon of daywear.

Left *Models in dresses by Henry Rosenfeld striking a pose with the designer himself. Rosenfeld was a budget label that offered well-cut and simply tailored dresses. His designs were an affordable example of the American Look, which often took Paris as its inspiration but adapted to be more comfortable and user-friendly versions.*

cufflinks), which had commenced with the appearance of Dior stockings in the late Forties, became an increasingly important economic aspect of Haute Couture. The result of these new production and dissemination initiatives was twofold: on the one hand, they helped reaffirm, if not extend, Paris's power; on the other, Haute Couture became more democratic and widely disseminated through increasingly better copies and an average salary now permitted many women to be elegantly dressed in the latest Parisian styles.

Out with the Old...

The favouring of ease and relative comfort without forgoing luxury became increasingly central to fashion as the decade drew to a close. The introduction of the Sack or Chemise dress by Givenchy and Balenciaga in 1957 – a straight, body-skimming, waistless dress inspired according to its creator by avant-garde art – caused a controversy not witnessed since Dior's 1947 collection. Despite its success, for

This meant that thousands upon thousands of copies of a Parisian model could be in circulation through department stores and ready-to-wear companies, either marketed as 'models inspired by' or 'original Christian Dior copies', depending again on what fee had been paid to the couture house. This meant that the bastion of tradition that was Haute Couture was adapting to post-war markets by adopting or at least exploiting mass-market strategies and channels. Some couturiers, such as Jacques Fath, went one step further and signed contracts that saw them working directly for American wholesale manufacturers. Furthermore, licensing (the selling of a designer name to a wholesale manufacturer to use on products such as stockings, scarves or

many it proved too extreme; yet the next year Yves Saint Laurent (who was by this point leading Maison Dior after its founder's death in the autumn of the previous year) introduced the Trapeze line, which many considered even more extreme and which, as observed by several commentators, 'resembled children's dresses'. A year later Balenciaga's Baby-doll dress reinforced this accusation.

The Sack and Trapeze dresses de-emphasised women's curves and thus, to an extent, desexualised and, as some suggested, infantilised them; these silhouettes were certainly more youthful and favoured a flatter, thinner, younger body than those promoted at the outset of the decade.

While the mainstream press was outraged and more mature customers stuck with the earlier, more conventional styles, it seems the younger Parisian designers realised that the future and the survival of Haute Couture lay with their peers. These designers were increasingly turning their backs on conservative styles, which did not match their lifestyle, beliefs and aspirations. The youth, street and subcultural styles that had been blossoming on the streets of London, Rome and Paris (and which owed little to the output of the stuffy Haute Couture salons) were preparing their onslaught towards fashion domination: Youthquake was about to hit.

Opposite *Stocking factory worker, 1954. Dior stockings were heavily advertised in women's magazines and featured illustrations by Haute Couture's favourite artist, René Gruau. The stockings allowed women of all classes to own their own piece of Dior and capitalised on the brand's reputation for luxury and elegance.*

Above *Afternoon Trapeze line dresses (left and right) by Yves Saint Laurent for Dior, 1958. Trapeze dresses flared out dramatically from a fitted shoulder line, and thus resembled children's smocks, which together with the shorter hemline seemed to be the main objection of the press to the new shape.*

Hubert de Givenchy

silhouette, it had a younger and more playful feel to it owing to his fabric and print choices, including lace and his famous fruit prints (1953). A year after his debut collection, Givenchy met Cristóbal Balenciaga, whose avant-garde designs he greatly admired, and this meeting is reflected in Givenchy's change in design direction: while he did not abandon his more classic and 'in fashion' silhouettes, they were joined by pieces that played with volume, draping and straighter lines. This led to both designers introducing their own versions of a new line – the Sack dress, a loose dress without a waistline – in the second half of the decade. His preference for separates did not only offer women an alternative to more formal evening dress, it also paved the way for luxury ready-to-wear that was elegant yet relaxed. His career skyrocketed after he met Audrey Hepburn on the set of *Sabrina* in 1951, and he would go on to design the famous black dress she wore in *Breakfast at Tiffany's*.

Givenchy managed what few couturiers achieved: universal praise. Not only did the press and celebrities adore him, but traditional, conservative customers, just as much as younger ones, eagerly awaited his every new collection. It seems this approval from all corners of the spectrum may have been down to the fact that he sought design inspiration in both the elitist beau monde of Paris and the more avant-garde locales of New York's East Village, and managed to marry these extremes into wearable, chic and novel silhouettes. Givenchy retired from fashion in 1995.

French aristocrat Hubert de Givenchy had worked for various designers including Jacques Fath, Robert Piguet, Lucien Lelong and Elsa Schiaparelli before opening his own maison in 1952. At just 25 he was the youngest designer in Paris at the time, and his progressive ideas soon found favour with the young and avant-garde; his collections were some of the few in Paris that offered an alternative to the dominating, conservative rule of Dior. From the outset his collections were characterised by their use of cheaper fabrics such as raw cotton and the predominance of daywear separates such as tailored suits, skirts and blouses.

His first collection included his Bettina blouse, which was copied worldwide. His evening wear was elegant and, while initially it incorporated a New Look

Above *Hubert de Givenchy with his models preparing for his first collection.*

Opposite *Audrey Hepburn in a Givenchy ball gown created for her role in Billy Wilder's* Sabrina, *1953. Hepburn and Givenchy, who met owing to his involvement as costume designer for the film, remained life-long friends and he went on to design some of her most iconic looks, including the black dress she wore as Holly Golightly in* Breakfast at Tiffany's, *1961.*

Cristóbal Balenciaga

Above *Cristóbal Balenciaga, photographed in 1950.*

Opposite *Silk wool gabardine coat, Balenciaga, 1950. This coat with gathered pleated sleeves is an exemplary example of Balenciaga's meticulous and structural approach to tailoring and his love of the interplay between the body, shape and volume.*

Cristóbal Balenciaga was a Basque-Spanish couturier whose idiosyncratic design vision, innovative cutting and tailoring techniques (which, unlike most of his contemporaries, he was able to execute himself) and reputation as a perfectionist earned him high praise from his contemporaries: Dior called him 'the master of us all... the only couturier in the truest sense of the word'.

Balenciaga was born into fashion – his mother was a seamstress and, at the age of 12, he began his tailoring apprenticeship. He later moved to Madrid where he trained formally. In 1919 he opened his first boutique in San Sebastián, and later opened branches in Madrid and Barcelona. The Spanish Civil War forced the closure of his business and he moved to Paris, where in 1937 he opened his Haute Couture salon.

While his early work showed innovation, it was not until the Fifties that his true design genius manifested itself in his collections, which by this point showed a near-complete disregard for the prevailing fashions of the day and instead presented original and conceptual silhouettes. Balenciaga's designs were often inspired by historical costume (Infanta dress) or traditional garments (he often used religious dress as inspiration), yet never felt old-fashioned. He favoured fluid, clean lines and bold colours – he was interested in the way the body related to clothes and how this could be changed by creating space between dress and body (unlike Dior and his followers, whose clothes were practically glued to the female body).

In 1951 Balenciaga transformed the silhouette by dispensing with curved shoulders and instead presenting broadened coats without a waist (see page 120). This streamlined and linear silhouette became his hallmark and attracted a loyal group of fanatical customers. His other innovations include the Balloon coat (1953), the Tunic dress (earliest version 1955), the high-waisted Baby-doll dress (1957), the Cocoon coat (1957), the Sack and Chemise dresses (1957 and 1958) and Empire-line coats and dresses (1959).

While his Sack and Chemise dresses were widely copied by ready-to-wear companies, Balenciaga was never a universally popular couturier in terms of sales, yet he was venerated by the press. His avant-garde designs were admired by many but bought by a loyal few, as they were genuinely different. However, his influence on fashion is immeasurable and many designers have cited him as their inspiration; this is clearly visible in the work of the Japanese and Belgian designers of the Eighties who, like Balenciaga, played with volume and did not wish to be restricted by the natural body in their designs. On his death in 1972, *Women's Wear Daily* ran the headline 'The King is Dead' – no further explanation was needed.

Pierre Balmain

The house became known for its daytime classics, but especially for its opulent and luxurious evening gowns that earned him the press title 'the king of French fashion'. Like those of his contemporaries, his designs had a sculptural quality that presented an uber-feminine essence. His use of luxurious silk brocades gave the dresses a shape of their own, yet he offset their stiffness through layering with delicate laces and with the resplendent finery and exquisite embroideries for which the house was most famous. His sophistication was particularly popular in the USA, where his designs were felt to embody Parisian ladylike chic – the perfect 1950s *jolie madame*. He capitalised on this reputation by selling ready-to-wear lines in America that earned him the Neiman Marcus Fashion Award in 1955.

By the Sixties he had started presenting more pared-down shapes in line with the current fashion, yet he continued to make extravagant evening wear for theatre and film productions, for Hollywood actresses, and most famously for Queen Sirikit of Thailand, who all continued to turn to him for gowns befitting award ceremonies or official occasions. While Balmain was no exceptional design innovator, his version of Parisian elegance summed up a decade, and furthermore his international outlook and early ventures in ready-to-wear marked him out as a truly modern designer.

Pierre Balmain was studying architecture at the Ecole des Beaux-Arts in Paris in 1934 when he was offered a job by Edward Molyneux. He had already undertaken some freelance design drawing work for Robert Piguet in previous years, but his post at Molyneux saw him abandon his studies. After five years, he joined Lucien Lelong and worked throughout the war alongside Christian Dior.

Balmain opened his own house in 1945, a veritable year of crisis for the Haute Couture industry, yet his initial collection was one of the few that managed to attract favourable reviews – the most famous and arguably most influential one written by his friend Gertrude Stein. He showcased long cloche skirts and small waists, hinting at things to come. His elegant yet wearable clothes gained him immediate success and celebrity customers including the Duchess of Windsor.

Above *Pierre Balmain fitting an Haute Couture dress on actress Ruth Ford, 1947.*

Opposite *Brigitte Bardot trying on a dress by Balmain for the film* La Mariée est Trop Belle *(1956). The creation exemplifies the conservative romantic opulence Balmain was known for; the dress features an embroidered bodice and a sumptuous bustled skirt reminiscent of the 1870s.*

The Cocktail Dress

● In the Thirties, Parisian designers including Schiaparelli and Patou presented dressy cocktail suits as separates for evening transition wear.

● During the Forties, out of necessity, the hemline of cocktail dresses was forced to rise from its original ankle length.

— Dior, in 1948, was the first to name an early-evening dress as a cocktail dress. This spurred on fashion retailers and magazines to start marketing and naming garments and accessories as 'cocktail'. The model here wears a black cocktail dress and black velvet wide-brimmed hat, designed by Ronald Paterson in 1955. The dress is clearly inspired by Dior's 1947 New Look silhouette and it was a shape that remained a favourite for cocktail dresses throughout the Fifties.

— Fifties cocktail dresses often featured long or midi sleeves or, if a dress had short or no sleeves, it was paired with a matching jacket. Dresses might have a modest neckline and were either closely fitted to the body or, more commonly, had full, New Look-style skirts. Fabrics and decoration tended to be plainer than those used for formal evening wear; the hemline was below the knee or calf-length, in contrast to floor-length evening wear.

While the history of the cocktail dress predates the Fifties by some decades, it was at this point that it became extremely popular among various classes and took on, in the minds of both designers and consumers, a more fixed look associated with a well-defined social function.

By the late Twenties, shifting social norms meant that women were not only able to partake more freely in public and social life, but that they could also drink without incurring disrepute. It is thus no coincidence that it is at this time that a fashion for private cocktail soirées emerged among the elite. Though the parties were not wholly formal, women preferred to wear sheath dresses with matching shoes, gloves and hats for these occasions. Compared with the Americans the French approached the affair in a much more relaxed manner: beach pyjamas, donned at the end of the day before changing into formal evening dress, were appropriate attire for the event; alternatively, informal sheath or shirt dresses were worn.

The cocktail party became a widespread pastime during the Fifties and couturiers all proposed their vision of appropriate attire.

1950s

The Chanel Suit

Upon her return from Switzerland in 1953, Coco Chanel was dismayed to find women once again shackled by restrictive skirts, jackets and undergarments in pursuit of fashion. She despised the fact that men had seemingly undone the sartorial advances she had helped to instigate in previous decades. To relaunch her couture house she approached her former business partner Pierre Wertheimer for capital and presented her new collection the following year.

That collection included several distinctive styles that are now fashion classics, such as long-stranded necklaces of artificial white pearls and the iconic quilted leather Chanel bag. It also saw the arrival of the Chanel suit with its famed cardigan jacket. Chanel's jersey suit of the late Teens and early Twenties had proved to be a true game-changer, and her Fifties suit would repeat that success.

The jacket became a staple of the house's collections, and while it was updated each season the basic pattern remained largely unchanged. Chanel once again became the embodiment and promoter of her own design – for the rest of her life she was rarely photographed without her tweed suit, presenting herself as an independent, elegant and successful woman who would not be tied down by restrictive fashions, and she encouraged other women to do the same. The Chanel suit has remained a constant at Maison Chanel and the cardigan jacket is a bestseller to this day.

— The Chanel suit's collarless jacket was made of bouclé tweed and was meant to be worn open. This cream-coloured jacket, with its four pockets that sat between the waist and the hips, was edged in knitted navy yarn, or decorated with contrasting trim. Like Chanel's jersey jackets, this suit jacket was barely structured and hung straight down instead of being fitted, as was the predominant vogue of the time.

⊕ Throughout the Fifties, versions with a collar, with brass buttons, and in a wide colour palette of plain or checked bouclé, either trimmed or plain, were proposed. Under the jacket a silk blouse or a jersey turtleneck were worn, and a matching skirt completed the suit; a scarf could be worn to accessorise.

— In contrast to the fashion of the time, Chanel proposed a subtle A-line knee-length wrap-over skirt, with or without a small kick pleat. Dresses in matching bouclé were also available; their cut, like that of the skirts, was rather straight and the dress itself oozed elegance in its plainness.

The Blouse

Blouses had formed part of the fashionable female wardrobe since the 1890s (although they had been worn as informal wear since the 1860s) and had indeed been key pieces at various times: the lingerie blouse of the opening decade of the century, the more masculine shirts of World War One, the sailor-style, cravat and Peter Pan blouses of the Twenties and the utilitarian shirt blouse of the Forties are just a few notable styles. However, in the Fifties the blouse gained in popularity.

During the 1940s, separates had been popularised and women's wardrobes had become more versatile because of this. Outfits could be easily updated by changing the less costly elements, so while a skirt could be the staple garment, wearing different blouses allowed a woman to vary her look. During the Fifties young women in particular enjoyed increased educational and employment opportunities, and for this they needed appropriately professional dress.

The blouse in effect became the female counterpart of the male shirt, which had been worn with the three-piece suit since the nineteenth century. Combined with a formal skirt and a cardigan or jacket, a blouse made for feminine, elegant and suitably serious professional attire.

—— Shoulders were rounded, soft and drooping, and sleeves were cleverly cut to achieve this. Collars and necklines came in a whole host of shapes but were always demure.

—— Fifties blouses ranged from the plain to the frivolous and could have full-, half- or quarter-length sleeves (for informal summer and holiday wear they could be sleeveless); they could be buttoned or wrap-around.

—— One of the most popular styles of the time was the Bettina blouse, launched by Givenchy in 1952. Named after Bettina Graziani (pictured), one of Paris's top models of the decade, the blouse was made of shirting and had a wide, open neck and full, ruffled broderie-anglaise sleeves, the ruffs going from the cuffs to the elbow. The blouse was meant to be teamed with a high-waisted pencil skirt and was immortalised by leading fashion illustrator René Gruau.

1960s

The A-line silhouette that had been introduced in the closing years of the Fifties by Balenciaga and later Saint Laurent de-emphasised female curves and consequently desexualised women, according to the male press. The new silhouette had also ushered in a new beauty ideal: instead of the more curvaceous 'grown-up' body, with a clearly defined waist, bust and hips, this new dress shape called for a taller, younger and flatter body. The press had cried 'infantalisation', and traditional couture costumers did their best to ignore the style, but, as the Sixties would prove, variations on this new line were here to stay.

One could argue that this late-Fifties silhouette was a first sign of youth fashions influencing high fashion. Youth had had its own fashion before the Sixties, but it was in this decade that its influence went mainstream and its ideas and aesthetics dominated fashion: this was the Youthquake decade.

The Kids Are Alright

The growing influence of youth culture was a direct consequence of World War Two and the baby boom that accompanied its ending. By the start of the Sixties, teenagers made up a significant part of the population, and as their politics, morals and lifestyles were often very different from those of their parents, they looked for fashions that could signal this difference. The thriving entertainment and music industry specifically courted and targeted this demographic, realising that they had disposable income and few commitments: they were the ideal consumers. Fashion did not lag behind, and throughout the decade increasing numbers of boutiques opened that catered to every different style and taste for the multiple youth tribes that began to proliferate.

Unlike high fashion, the epicentre of youth fashion in the Sixties was London. The city's vibrant music and arts scene, in combination with the growing rejection of the

oppressive class system by the post-war generation, heavily influenced the development of different youth cultures, each with its own recognisable sartorial style.

Young designers such as Mary Quant, often without any formal training, had been working on creating clothes that were fun and exciting and, most importantly, different from what their parents wore. Quant and many others wanted young people to have fashions all of their own. But while the streets, cafés and clubs of London were a hive of sartorial experimentation, established Parisian couturiers mostly ignored young people and their alternative looks; the young were not their main customers, nor were they considered sophisticated or elitist enough to be style leaders.

Above *During the Sixties London's Carnaby Street became one of the youth hotspots and home to boutiques, including Mates, Lady Jane, Carnaby Girl, Lord John and John Stephen. In fact the street mostly specialised in menswear; Kings Road in Chelsea was where the more famous womenswear boutiques were found.*

Left *London designer Mary Quant sporting her famous and much-copied bob created by Vidal Sassoon.*

Street Style

André Courrèges claimed to have been the 'inventor' of the miniskirt; however, ample evidence suggests that Mary Quant had been selling miniskirts in her boutique Bazaar prior to Courrèges. Unlike Courrèges, Quant had no desire to claim its invention and ascribed the fashion item to 'the girls on the streets of Chelsea'.

Quant's crediting of youth culture with the emergence of new fashion not only affirmed the now indisputable influence of youth fashions on Haute Couture through the bubbling up of youth styles, it also signalled the end of the traditional dictatorial fashion system. No longer did the economic and class elite simply dictate what their perceived social inferiors should wear; now the young, free and experimental wielded considerable power.

Left *Models wearing Courrèges minidresses, Life Magazine, 1968.*

Counter-Couture

There were, however, a few more visionary designers who could see the writing was on the wall for the traditional couture system. They set about rejuvenating Haute Couture by changing design and production methods and attempting to infuse the industry with all the excitement and experimentation that was happening on the streets of London.

Yves Saint Laurent was a principal player in this high-fashion revolution. Having introduced the shocking and youthful A-line in the previous decade, he went one step further in 1960 and presented his Beat collection

for Maison Dior. Beat was short for 'beatnik', the post-war dropout generation of American writers Jack Kerouac and Allen Ginsberg, who questioned conventional society and materialism, promoted the use of mind-altering drugs, and whose ideas were closely aligned to French Left Bank existentialism. Beats were cool, young, alternative and most certainly not Haute Couture. Saint Laurent's collection included knitted turtlenecks, black leather jackets, a crocodile-skin jacket with a mink collar, fur jackets with knitted sleeves, and a helmet-like hat of mink fur, a nod to biker culture. The press (both in France and abroad) was confused at best and outraged at worst at this sartorial ode to what polite society considered a dangerous counterculture.

However shocking Saint Laurent's decision to look at young people in the street for inspiration may have been, in retrospect it proved a monumental shift as it showed that youth styles could be reworked into elegant and luxurious garments for older Haute Couture clients.

Opposite *Yves Saint Laurent in 1969, posing with two models outside his Rive Gauche store on Bond Street, London, which stocked his ready-to-wear line of the same name. The model on the left, Betty Catroux, is wearing Saint Laurent's famous 1968 safari jacket as a minidress.*

The Revolutionary Mini

Another objection levelled against the Beat look was the amount of leg on show – not from the moral perspective, but because, as fashion magazines pointed out, only the young and slender had limbs that could carry off these shorter skirts. These cries fell on deaf ears, and in the next three years hemlines crept up further, to unprecedented heights: the miniskirt became the emblem of all that was youthful in fashion.

From a cultural perspective, the appearance and popularity of the miniskirt is often linked to the availability of the contraceptive pill and the sexual revolution this instigated: women were now in control of their own bodies and could more freely engage in non-reproductive relations outside marital unions. The miniskirt and minidress resexualised women, but in an almost Lolita-esque manner – the cut and bright colours were nearly childlike, yet never before had women's thighs been on display. The result was to many oddly unsettling, and whereas the press had lamented the desexualisation of women only a few years earlier, they were now outraged at the audacity of it all. It was not uncommon for young women to be hissed or spat at in the street.

Opposite *Metal Plate Armour dress, Paco Rabanne, 1967. Rabanne's Sixties designs were characterised by experimentation with new, often non-luxury, materials such as plastic paillettes, aluminium and Rhodoid plates and discs. Chanel remarked: 'he's not a couturier, he's a metal worker'. Rabanne also created more wearable versions of his space-age look that were infinitely more comfortable (the metal dresses were heavy and cold) and much cheaper, because although he used 'everyday' materials such as plastic and aluminium the production process was lengthy and costly.*

Futuristic Fashions

The apparent shift in fashion influence from Parisian Haute Couture houses to London boutiques did not mean that garments from each were considered equal. The Parisian garments were superior in material and construction and infinitely more sophisticated in conception and design; if this had not been the case, Paris would have struggled to justify its exorbitant prices. Whereas many of the London boutique creations were made of cheap, often man-made fibres, French designer André Courrèges's Sixties creations, however simple in cut, nearly always featured intricate detailing of appliqué work, and Saint Laurent continued to use luxury pelts and hides.

One type of man-made 'fabric' that did enter the lexicon of couture was what would be deemed futuristic or space-age materials, such as plastics (especially the Paco Rabanne-favoured Mylar) and metallics. These new fashion elements allowed for previously unseen design possibilities and perfectly fitted in with the Sixties' space race obsession. In 1964, Courrèges unleashed his Moon Girl dressed in geometric, almost architectural, tailored garments in a futuristic palette of white and silver with bright red, vivid pink and orange detailing in lacquered and PVC-coated fabrics. His dropped-waist minidresses were worn with double-breasted coats, helmet-shaped hats and go-go boots. French designer Francisco Rabaneda Cuervo (better known as Paco Rabanne) presented his futuristic woman clad in a chain-mail dress of silver and black paillettes, the peephole effect of which showed off the wearer's body underneath. Italian-born Pierre Cardin presented bright block-coloured dresses with matching tights and lacquered leather and PVC boots, space-travel capes in innovative cuts and tightly clinging, finely knitted bodysuits. In 1968, even Queen Elizabeth II's couturier Hardy Amies designed his version of this space cadet when he provided the costumes for Stanley Kubrick's *2001: A Space Odyssey*; however, his space ladies were extraordinarily demure compared to the sex-kitten PVC and Perspex costumes

worn by Jane Fonda as *Barbarella* in the same year, whose on-screen garments (on the few occasions she wore any in the film) were directly inspired by Rabanne.

Peace, Love and Haute Couture

While space travel and an optimistic view of the future dominated much of style innovation in the Sixties, these were not the only cultural influences translated into fashion. Art, especially Op and Pop Art, also provided valuable sources of inspiration: Saint Laurent's wool-jersey Mondrian dress of 1965 spawned millions of home-made and ready-to-wear copies, and his 1966 Pop Art collection of brightly coloured dresses was inspired by Andy Warhol's screen-prints of everyday consumer objects.

This nod to mass consumer culture, albeit via contemporary art, not only showed off his sensibility for the modern and the 'here and now', but also signalled his underlying dissatisfaction with the traditional Haute Couture system and its elitist nature, not least its pricing.

To attract younger customers, Saint Laurent launched his ready-to-wear line Rive Gauche (Left Bank) in 1966, its name clearly signalling where its design and price ethos resided (the Left Bank of the Seine was where 'alternative' thinkers would congregate). This move was met with complete shock and horror by the more established houses, but he defended his decision by stating that ready-to-wear was not sub-couture but the future. Time would prove him right.

In the mid-Sixties, America saw the rise of hippy culture, which spread quickly among the young, culminating in the 1967 Summer of Love and the 1969 Woodstock festival. Hippies, like the beats before them, rejected materialism and Western values, and their politics were reflected through their anti-fashions: both men and women dressed in Asian-inspired garb of tunics, beads and flowing maxi dresses (often in bright colours or featuring exotic or psychedelic prints) or jeans and T-shirts to signal their questioning of gender roles. They moved both the political and sexual revolution forward and their ideas spread to Europe,

where, mixed in with existentialist rhetoric, they culminated in the Paris Spring of 1968. Saint Laurent went out into the streets to sketch young protesters on the barricades and, inspired by their demands, designed a collection of trouser suits for women, including his now iconic safari suit for the urban female warrior. In the same year Sonia Rykiel, who had started making upmarket ready-to-wear in the early Sixties, opened her boutique in Saint-Germain on the Left Bank, where she sold clinging knitwear designed to be worn without a bra. Freedom of bodies, sexuality and a relaxing of moral codes were embodied by her designs, which she defined as woman-friendly. Traditional values and gender roles were being questioned if not overturned, and fashion traced and contributed to this journey.

Breaking New Ground

Hippy politics were not the only thing to make it across the ocean – the fashions were also creeping in, albeit in a luxurious manner that conveniently overlooked the movement's rejection of wealth, class and taste. The 1969 couture collections saw lowered hemlines, colourful prints, floaty fabrics and exotic elements replace the starkly modern architectural space-age look.

While Saint Laurent presented multicoloured patchwork maxi dresses for his 1969 collection, on the whole London was faster in the uptake of these hippy-luxe fashions. British designers such as Celia Birtwell, Ossie Clark and Zandra Rhodes, as well as ready-to-wear label turned cult brand Biba, all embraced the new aesthetic. But the real leaders, if not pioneers, had been the post-war Italian luxury ready-to-wear brands like Pucci and Missoni, whose printed and knitted creations respectively were the perfect combination of innovation, luxury and colour.

The Sixties marked a period of profound change in all spheres of life and this was clearly reflected and documented in the fashions. This created a new and fruitful relationship between Haute Couture and youth culture, which ensured that Paris retained its influence but now, instead of setting the tone, increasingly

followed, appropriated and adapted what was created on
the streets of London and Saint-Germain. Young people
were forging a new future and Paris did not want to be
left out. Realising that the restrictive pricing of Haute
Couture would never accommodate the young, Yves Saint
Laurent fully embraced the ready-to-wear market and
in so doing laid the foundations for our contemporary
designer brand obsession, creating not just a new product
but also a new market alongside it.

This bubbling up of styles and the introduction of
innovative ready-to-wear meant that by the end of the
decade the definition of fashion itself had been widened
and democratised, and the fashion landscape was now
infinitely richer, more diverse and inclusive.

Above *Models dressed in hippy fashions,
London, 1967. The American hippy movement
was quick to spread to London and psychedelic,
ethnic and peasant styles were quickly taken up
by young urbanites.*

Pierre Cardin

The Italian-born Pierre Cardin moved to Paris in 1945. During his first few years in the city he worked for various couture houses, including Paquin and Schiaparelli, before settling at the newly established Maison Dior in late 1946. Cardin is believed to have helped Dior create his ultra-feminine Corolle line, which is ironic given that for the rest of his independent career Cardin focused on making comfortable, linear and comparatively plain clothes. He left Dior in 1950 to set up his own company that specialised in stage costume; however, soon, with the aid of Dior, he started attracting private clients who wanted him to design their wardrobes.

The business quickly grew and three years later Cardin became a member of the Chambre Syndicale and a licensed Haute Couturier. A year after that he opened his first boutique and presented his bubble dresses: loose-fitting gowns that were tightened at the waist and gathered either at the top or bottom to create a bubble effect. The silhouette was young and different – it did away with the stifled, lady-like look of Dior

yet avoided the almost snobbish intellectualism of Balenciaga. Cardin continued to experiment with shape and volume, yet his clothes always remained wearable.

In 1959 he was temporarily expelled from the Chambre Syndicale, supposedly because he was selling a ready-to-wear line in Printemps, the Paris department store. He was reinstated the following year, but the incident showed where Cardin's true interest lay and that indeed he was ahead of the pack in seeing the mass market and not private clients as the future of fashion.

The Sixties was a varied, productive and successful decade for Cardin; his style became increasingly linear and clean (he favoured tunics above all else), he experimented with colour blocking and, most famously, he became a leading promoter of the space-age look. These futuristic creations often employed geometric shapes as motifs, and used new materials in their construction, including vinyl and other plastics, silver and patent leathers and large zipper fastenings. Cardin even created plastic goggles and helmets to finish off the look. His designs were sold extensively throughout the Sixties and by the end of the decade his fame was such that he could go on to license a diverse range of products to carry his name, including furniture, cars, cookware and cosmetics.

Though Cardin's use of licensing attracted much criticism from his competitors, he was one of the first to understand, and indeed capitalise on, the power of the designer name and product, which has become the standard practice and financially underpins today's fashion industry.

Above *Pierre Cardin capitalised on the designer name, expanding his interests into industrial design with products bearing his signature and logo – here an executive jet.*

Opposite *Pierre Cardin with his models wearing designs from his Sixties space-age collection including his famous helmet hats and wide, oilcloth belts.*

Emilio Pucci

Above *Emilio Pucci with models in 1962. Pucci's unlined, relaxed designs in bright coloured prints made him a favourite of the jet-setting elite and saw his styles copied extensively.*

Opposite *Model photographed on the roof of Palazzo Pucci in Florence wearing a matching bikini and wrap-around skirt, part of Pucci's 1965 Spring/Summer collection.*

Emilio Pucci was an aristocratic Florentine fashion designer whose textile designs and comfortable flowing and draped creations attracted worldwide fame during the Sixties.

Pucci, a keen skier, had started by designing skiwear in the Forties. Initially this was purely a sportswear undertaking, but when in 1947 a *Harper's Bazaar* photographer spotted his designs, he was commissioned to design skiwear for a winter fashion shoot, which was run the following year. His designs executed in stretch fabrics (still considerably novel at the time) were a sensation and offers by US manufacturers poured in.

Pucci then opened a fashion boutique on the island of Capri. His first collections focused on swimwear, owing to his understanding of stretch fabrics. However, encouraged by US retailers he soon extended his range to include scarves, blouses and wrinkle-free dresses, all featuring the trademark Pucci prints in a kaleidoscope of colours. The relaxed nature of his designs and the vivid colour palette marked them out as different and original in the late Forties; they quickly proved a hit with the international jet-setting elite. Pucci's presence on the island boosted Capri's appeal as a tourist destination, and he soon opened a second boutique in Rome.

By the early Fifties, Pucci was receiving international awards. He was particularly popular in the USA, as his clothes were in line with American post-war sportswear fashions. But it was in the Sixties that he became a household name as the likes of Marilyn Monroe, Sophia Loren and Jackie Kennedy were photographed wearing his creations. His patterns, his relaxed, unlined, casual designs in lightweight fabrics such as silk and jersey, and his colour palette perfectly captured the decade's mood. Pucci designed all his own prints, drawing inspiration from architecture, history and far-flung cultures, and they became synonymous with casual chic.

As evidence of his popularity, Pucci was asked to design the Braniff International Airways hostesses' and pilots' uniforms; this commission saw him create

the bubble helmet, a clear plastic helmet worn by flight attendants between the aircraft and the terminal building to protect their hairdos. His designs were so well received that he ended up designing six complete uniform collections for the company between 1965 and 1974; even Barbie had versions of the uniform. Pucci mania reached its pinnacle in 1967 but the company continues to produce its trademark prints with global success.

Yves Saint Laurent

Algerian-born French designer Yves Saint Laurent moved to Paris at the age of 18 to enrol at the Chambre Syndicale. His designs quickly got him noticed and an introduction by Michel De Brunhoff, the editor of French *Vogue*, secured him a job at Maison Dior. When Dior died unexpectedly in 1957, the 21-year-old Saint Laurent found himself head designer at the house. His first Dior collection introduced the Trapeze line – essentially a much plainer, pared-down version of the New Look – and catapulted him to international fashion stardom.

His following collections, however – in particular the Beat-inspired Left Bank fashions – were almost universally panned by the fashion press. In 1960, Saint Laurent was conscripted to serve with the French Army in the Algerian War of Independence, but he lasted a mere 20 days before being admitted to a military hospital suffering from stress. Adding insult to injury, it was here that he found out he had been fired and replaced at Dior. After his release from the army he successfully sued Dior for breach of contract and set up his own fashion house: Yves Saint Laurent (YSL).

No longer catering to an older, more conservative Dior client, his youthful and innovative designs soon attracted loyal followers and the majority of his collections were well received by the press.

In 1966, he was the first couturier to offer a wholly stand-alone prêt-à-porter line, Rive Gauche, in its own designated store (others before him had offered ready-to-wear separates as part of their couture collection). Saint Laurent understood that ready-to-wear was the future, and while he adored Haute Couture for the fantasy licence it offered his design skills, he wanted good design to be more democratic and available to a much wider audience. French actress Catherine Deneuve, whose wardrobe for Luis Buñuel's *Belle de Jour* he ended up designing a year later, became the unofficial godmother of the store.

While his Sixties couture collections were often inspired by modern art (the Mondrian dress 1965, Warhol and Wesselmann-inspired Pop Art collection 1966) and regularly included lavish decorations (including feathers, sequins, beading and embroidery) and bold prints, his Rive Gauche creations were modern and sleek. His most notable collections and pieces of the decade included the 1967 African collection, his 1968 safari jacket and, most importantly, his 1966 Smoking (tuxedo suit) for women. Although Chanel had suggested trousers as leisurewear decades earlier, Saint Laurent's suit now gave women a day- and evening-wear version, blurring gender boundaries and affording women the ultimate in comfort.

Yves Saint Laurent remained a fashion great until the late Seventies, when his popularity started to diminish, but his influence and importance in both design and business terms still resonate today.

Opposite *The abstract paintings of Piet Mondrian are clearly referenced in this day dress (centre) designed by Yves Saint Laurent in 1965.*

Left *Model wearing an Yves Saint Laurent camel-coloured coat with a button and bow fastening, a straight skirt and a nutria fur hat, 1962. After his departure from Dior, YSL was able to freely present more youthful Haute Couture styles as he was keen to revive the industry by attracting a younger audience.*

Hippy Chic

The second half of the decade witnessed young people worldwide rebel politically, socially and, consequently, sartorially. One such set of young people, the hippies – a name purportedly given to them by the journalist Herb Caen who worked for the *San Francisco Chronicle* – would come to have significant influence on mainstream fashion in the closing years of the Sixties.

Hippies were, in many ways, an updated version of the Fifties beats. Their countercultural values saw them create their own style, language, music and communities. Pacifist in nature and committed to the promotion of universal love, they rejected consumerism and Western values and instead embraced mind-altering drugs in pursuit of personal and societal liberation and growth. In 1967, thousands of hippies descended on San Francisco's Haight-Ashbury district, leading to the Summer of Love and culminating in the infamous 1969 Woodstock festival.

Indeed, music was instrumental in bringing hippy influences to high and consequently mainstream fashion. Rock and pop acts such as the Beatles, Jimi Hendrix, Janis Joplin and Joni Mitchell put these counterculture looks in the spotlight and, while high fashion was initially reluctant, the look was soon adopted, albeit in a more polished and luxurious manner. London was quicker off the mark than Paris (partly because hippy fashions had some of their roots in British Mod styles), and boutiques such as Granny Takes a Trip, Hung on You, Mr Freedom and I Was Lord Kitchener's Valet sold a variety of different hippy and psychedelic styles. Upmarket versions, known as hippy luxe, hippy chic or boho chic, were equally available.

—— Twiggy wearing a printed flowing maxi dress by Bill Gibb with knitted cap, c. 1970. Hippy fashions were colourful (patterned or tie-dyed) and comfortable, incorporating many utilitarian garments such as jeans, T-shirts and vest tops. Midi and maxi dresses and skirts were favoured over the popular mini.

⊕ Non-Western garments such as dashikis, kaftans and ponchos were popular for men and women, as were Native American jewellery, beaded necklaces and head scarves.

⊕ In 1968 Zandra Rhodes opened the Fulham Road Clothes Shop where she sold loose, billowing chiffon garments in her trademark colourful prints inspired by far-flung places and cultures, which were perfectly in tune with the times. Celia Birtwell and Ossie Clark sold their modern yet romantic gowns of silk chiffon, jersey or crêpe de Chine from their Quorum boutique. Only in 1969, when Yves Saint Laurent lowered hemlines and included patchwork-printed maxi dresses, did Paris catch up. The look then became mainstream and went on to dominate the opening years of the Seventies.

The Miniskirt and Minidress

In the late Fifties Balenciaga, Givenchy and Yves Saint Laurent had started raising hemlines with their chemise dresses and the Trapeze line, again to vocal objection from more conservative customers and press. However, those rises would be seen as minimal compared to the dizzying heights to which skirts would creep in the Sixties. During the first three years of the decade hemlines kept rising under the lead of Parisian elite designers, London self-trained boutique owners and, most importantly, young people trying to find a different, rebellious style.

While it is impossible and ultimately unimportant to settle the 'Who did it first?' debate (Mary Quant or Courrèges?), London models Twiggy (pictured opposite) and Jean Shrimpton became the unofficial miniskirt poster girls and the representatives of a new fashion ideal that was younger and slimmer than their predecessors. The mini was responsible for the demise of stockings, as they were inadequate at covering legs when worn with an ultra-short skirt. Instead, tights (pantyhose) were needed, and these now came in all colours of the rainbow; the more savvy brands such as Quant and Biba, spotting a gap in the market, were quick to license their own ranges.

The mini remained popular with the young for the duration of the Sixties, but when the hemlines were dropped again in Paris and London in the closing year of the decade, its days were numbered.

Twiggy wearing a pink A-line minidress. Its shape attracted much criticism from the traditional press when introduced in the late Fifties, as it was felt it infantilised women. Young women on the other hand were fast in its uptake and variants of the style (colour and sleeve styles) remained popular throughout the Sixties.

Alongside miniskirts, minidresses (either straight shifts, A-line or trapeze-shaped) were a firm favourite with young women, who teamed them with brightly coloured tights and chunky high-heeled sandals or boots.

⊕ In Paris, Cardin and Courrèges offered miniskirts and dresses in bright space-age colours and in experimental fabrics. In London, Mary Quant and John Bates retailed a wide variety of minis inspired by Op and Pop Art shapes and palettes. Even Biba, Barbara Hulanicki's boutique, better remembered for its ethereal retro maxi gowns, sold minidresses in Art Nouveau prints or polka dots with voluminous sleeves and Peter Pan collars.

Le Smoking

Yves Saint Laurent | 1966

Created by Yves Saint Laurent in 1966 as part of his Pop Art collection, Le Smoking was the first designer tuxedo for women. Of course, women had worn tuxedos in the past – most famously Marlene Dietrich in *Morocco* (1930) – but this was more about transgression and titillation than fashion. Suits, in general, were not uncommon for women, although trouser suits were still very rare and only worn by the very young, daring or avant-garde. What made Saint Laurent's version so important and influential was the fact that it presented a long, minimal style that was decidedly androgynous and thus afforded women the opportunity to wear clothes that had been exclusively reserved for powerful and/or wealthy men.

Though entirely accepted now, at the time of its inception Le Smoking was seen as a brazen assault on masculinity and femininity alike, but as its shock appeal wore off its importance grew. Le Smoking remains a favourite of ordinary women and celebrities alike, and can be seen year upon year on the red carpet, where it still manages to attract the attention of the press.

—— This designer tailored suit paved the way for the Eighties Power suit and can be seen in retrospect as a symbol of growing female emancipation. In many ways it represented a modern version of the Twenties Little Black Dress (which had similarly been representative of newly empowered femininity), in line with Sixties ideas on gender equality and second-wave feminism.

—— The image and the outfit were sexual but both relied on a far more masculine, angular and empowered sexuality than was the norm: no cuteness, no frilliness, no conventional femininity.

⊕ In 1970 the suit's popularity rocketed when Bianca Macias married Mick Jagger in Saint-Tropez wearing a white version of the tuxedo jacket over her bare body (though she wore it with a white skirt, not the trousers as is often misreported – she did however wear a white Smoking on other occasions). Thousands of women copied her look for their own special occasion.

1970s

The Sixties had introduced many fashion changes, not just in the realms of style, but more importantly in terms of consumer choice and accessibility. A rapidly developing and hugely popular ready-to-wear market that catered to all levels of society and incomes meant that fashion – but also luxury in the form of designer ready-to-wear – could now be bought off the peg.

That decade also witnessed how countercultural and youth styles, previously ignored by high fashion, had started being appropriated and incorporated into Haute Couture, and indeed constituted a big section of the designer ready-to-wear market in the second half of the decade, thus changing the power balance between fashion and the consumer.

The Seventies would pick up on this wave of choice and take it to a new level, creating an air of freedom and an anti-institutional ethos in its fashions. (I use the term 'fashions' because there is no one overarching fashion trend that defines the era; this fact, combined with the disintegration of Paris's supreme dictatorial power in matters of fashion and taste, resulted in a landscape that favoured a patchwork of influences and influencers.)

Rewriting the Rules

Many have interpreted the lack of a clear sartorial direction in the Seventies as confusion in a time of worldwide economic uncertainty triggered by successive oil crises; however, the absence of one clear look is arguably a sign of a fragmentation of the fashion system that was guided by personal choice rather than designers or journalists. This was the 'Me' decade, where consumers exercised their agency and constructed their own fashionable identity as they pleased. Even *Vogue* declared that 'There are no rules in the fashion game now.'

The midi hippy-luxe styles presented by Saint Laurent in 1969 (and embraced and promoted by London designers in the closing years of the Sixties) would set the sartorial tone for the opening years of the Seventies. Midi and maxi dresses in bright neo-Art

Left *The early Seventies saw the miniskirt, indelibly associated with the Sixties, give ground to the midi with its hippy associations.*

Nouveau or 'ethnic' prints joined the still-popular miniskirt in the lexicon of fashionable hemline options. The three jostled for pole position for several years with no clear winner emerging, because while high fashion went decidedly midi in the 1970s, ordinary women, particularly in America, were having none of it; the miniskirt had become a sign of youth and liberation in the Sixties and they were not about to do away with this visual marker just because Paris said '*Non*'.

Maxi skirts and dresses, however, did not quite spell the end of legs on display, as they often featured decency-defying splits right to the thigh.

1970s

Above *Liza Minnelli in Bob Fosse's 1972 film* Cabaret. *Set in Thirties Berlin the film tapped into the revival vogue of the Seventies. Its hit status proved a catalyst for the revivalist glamour fashions of the Seventies, as* The Great Gatsby *reintroduced Twenties-style dresses and jersey sportswear.*

The (slightly) longer skirt received a boost from Yves Saint Laurent in 1971, when he presented a collection heavily inspired by 1940s fashions. Among his creations on this occasion were a bright green boxy fox-fur jacket with exaggerated shoulders, big turbans, platform shoes and over-the-knee skirts and dresses. The whole look was reminiscent of louche wartime prostitutes. Traditional couture clients were outraged, but the fashion press went wild.

The same collection also featured floral tea dresses, which with Saint Laurent's endorsement became de rigueur for the first time since World War Two.

More Retro Inspiration

The 1940s were not the only decade to make a sartorial comeback in the Seventies. The film *Cabaret* (1972) glamorised Thirties decadence, and the London fashion store Biba spearheaded the revival of the look. Biba copied Thirties Hollywood glamour but added a dark, sexy and mysterious twist: figure-hugging bias-cut maxi dresses in champagne pink, gold and cobalt blue were teamed with leopard-print jackets or feather shrugs, and platform sandals or boots in matching colours. In Paris, interwar influences were also present in collections by Balmain, Mugler and Cardin.

The 1920s also enjoyed a revival, especially from 1974 onwards when *The Great Gatsby* opened in cinemas. While the costumes were clearly based on Twenties fashion, they had a distinctly contemporary feel about them and the film's popularity sparked a jazz-age trend; both catwalk and ready-to-wear collections delivered new versions of Twenties styles.

Others travelled back to early twentieth-century London and Paris by adopting the romanticised bohemian styles of artistic and literary circles: kimono- and Liberty-style dresses in crushed velvets were teamed with 'piano' shawls – large, square, silk-fringed and often embroidered – beaded necklaces and silk scarves or headscarves. This look became particularly popular in Britain, where resistance to longer skirts had been much less than in America.

An excessive use of pattern is another hallmark of the Seventies, and an abundance of choice in pattern and colour was available at both ends of the market. While the decade is often remembered for its most excessive and ostentatious prints, it has to be noted that aside from these multicoloured maxi patterns (as championed by Pucci or Rhodes), 1940s small floral and polka-dot prints were equally popular. Historic Art Nouveau or William Morris prints were given a contemporary twist

through the manipulation of scale and the introduction of a contemporary colour scheme, and the stylistic influences were drawn from everything from the 1880s to the 1950s.

One designer who particularly favoured late-Victorian designs was Laura Ashley, who created dresses and accessories out of printed cottons that featured small

Above *Twiggy at Biba's Kensington store in 1971. Biba offered figure-hugging bias-cut maxi dresses in champagne pink, gold, leek green and cobalt blue, sequinned halter-neck tops and dresses à la Vionnet, and leopard-print faux fur jackets. Accessories included ostrich-feather shrugs, gold and silver turbans, satin boudoir pyjamas as daywear, opera gloves and platform sandals.*

1880s calico prints. For her dress designs the Welsh designer turned to Edwardian England and her cotton dresses often featured ruffled hems, leg-of-mutton sleeves and lace inserts. These olde-worlde dresses were worn with printed calico headscarves to complete the pastoral Milkmaid look. In America, Ralph Lauren suggested something similar in the second half of the decade, referred to as the Prairie style.

The Nostalgia Effect

It is not in the actual designs but in the *reasons* for this historic dressing up that we find a truly novel idea underpinning Seventies fashion. The popularity of historic fantasy styles hints at both an escapist motive and the feeling that a generation who had missed out on the original party were trying to recreate it. Through this plundering of history we can discern a desire to recapture an authenticity of the past. By acknowledging that the past is authentic, one of course suggests that the present is not, and for the Seventies generation this attitude made complete sense. In the face of economic hardship, they found comfort and safety in a romanticised idea of the past. This borrowing was thus a potent form of nostalgia.

This Seventies nostalgia had two distinctly different faces: retro nostalgia and insular nostalgia. The former takes its cue from history but infuses it with irony and hence subverts its reference. For example, Yves Saint

Opposite *Selection of Laura Ashley peasant dresses at the 'Laura Ashley: Romantic heroine' exhibition, Bath, 2013. Ashley favoured ditsy Victorian calico prints and produced dresses and accessories in their original colours and modern palettes of lime green and bright red.*

Left *Models wearing variations of the same outfit showing the options now available to women. The Seventies saw the mainstream acceptance of trousers and, typical of the 'Me' ethos that dominated the decade, skirts came in various fashionable lengths.*

Laurent's adaptations of wartime fashions, which attracted criticisms of 'vulgarity', 'kitsch' and 'bad taste', can be seen as sartorial bricolage, laden with irony, subverting the past by addressing a problematic period in France's fashion history.

Insular nostalgia, on the other hand, presents a pastiche of the past that lacks all irony and humour. Instead of questioning history, it copies the past but makes it better. Laura Ashley's Edwardian peasant dresses presented a romanticised and sanitised version of a time that was marked by abject rural poverty.

Even though these two forms of nostalgia are radically different in their treatment of the past, both are evidence of a need for stability and certainty. In times of prosperity our view is optimistic, and in fashion this equates to looking towards the future; in times of crisis, however, the present (let alone the future) is a place out of our control, whereas the past is something we can shape to satisfy our contemporary needs.

Anxiety about the present was also expressed through cultural borrowing. Mexican peasant blouses, Indian scarves, colourful kaftans, embroidered djellabas and Eastern European folk embroidery all found their way into the Western wardrobe – in the same way that the past was romanticised, so too were foreign cultures.

La Femme Masculine

While this historic and cultural borrowing created some spectacular fashions, the most influential borrowing took place in a less ostentatious manner, from the male wardrobe. This happened in different ways, but arguably for similar reasons: greater gender equality and a desire for comfort for women. While many hallmarks of Seventies fashion can be interpreted as the erosion of strict gender codes, the most potent one has to be the mass adoption of trousers by women: tailored trousers for work and jeans for leisure. Jeans were very quickly co-opted into the fashion system and designer denim by Gloria Vanderbilt, Pierre Cardin and Calvin Klein was already undermining the equality proposed by this genderless and classless garment.

Equally, trouser suits appeared in numerous guises for both day and evening wear throughout the decade. Wide flares and belted tailored jackets were typical of early Seventies suits, but from the mid-Seventies onwards a less structured jacket became dominant owing to Italian designer Giorgio Armani's introduction of the looser style.

This trouser-suit look was soon termed the Dress for Success look, named after John T. Molloy's influential 1975 dress manual.

1970s

Never Mind the Couture

Whereas the first half of the decade was dominated by fantasy, retro, pastiche and ethnic styles, things changed dramatically in the second half. From 1975 through to late 1979, mainstream fashion became both more conservative and more severe. In youth and street fashions, the designer-hippy ethos of freedom and choice was followed by the nihilistic and shocking styles of punk, while the middle classes increasingly gravitated towards the uniformity of the Dress for Success look (signalling the advent of the dominant power-dressing look of the 1980s).

This shift by youth culture towards the violence and deliberate bad taste of punk fashions, and the middle classes' increasingly conservative look, were both born out of the same reasons: the deepening economic crisis, political upheaval and social fragmentation. But whereas the former chose to visually confront these social ills, the latter tried to adjust to them and fit in through the adoption of a uniform style.

In opposition to hippy youth culture style, punk clothes were generally black and deliberately menacing. Punks, like hippies before them, adopted a DIY ethos and either made their own clothes or bought second-hand garments, often customising them. For those on a more generous budget, Vivienne Westwood and Malcolm McLaren's boutique Seditionaries (originally called Sex) on the Kings Road in London sold ready-to-wear bondage trousers, T-shirts with sexually and politically explicit imagery, and deliberately 'ugly' mohair sweaters in garish colours.

While punk, with its extreme styles, had little impact on mainstream fashions, it had nevertheless picked up on the sinister and growing cultural undercurrent of (sexual) violence and brutality. On the catwalk, 'Terrorist Chic' made black leather stylish precisely because it evoked images of sadomasochistic sex, which was regarded as the last taboo. German designer Karl

A Softer Side

Disco's roots predate the Seventies, but it was around 1974 that it surged in popularity, culminating in 1977's *Saturday Night Fever* mania. Disco fashions originated in dancewear and therefore leotards, body stockings and shorts were essential elements of the look, as well as flowing and draped mini and maxi dresses that had a distinctive Grecian feel about them and allowed free movement of the body. Fashion designers were quick to capitalise on the look.

The soft, often draped and relatively unconstructed creations by American designer Roy Halston Frowick were particularly influential. He favoured the artificial fibre Ultrasuede and liquid jersey, and his fluid halter-neck jumpsuits, blouses, dresses and trousers were worn by the celebrities of the day in New York's ultra-trendy epicentre of disco, Studio 54. *Women's Wear Daily* gushed: 'The 1970s belong to Halston.'

The Seventies closed with a variety of styles that now all fell under the banner of Fashion; no single look came out victorious as being definitive of the era. The suit in all its different guises was the only fashion to have lasted the decade, and would take centre stage in the next.

Lagerfeld, as well as fashion photographers such as Helmut Newton and Guy Bourdin, disseminated the fetishistic style. A less sexualised version of brutality was proposed in the collections of Daniel Hechter, who dressed women in tweed suits teamed with black berets and leather coats that appeared to reference the IRA.

Opposite *New York's Studio 54, the world's most famous nightclub, became an instant success when it opened in 1977 with a strict dresscode: 'glamour only'.*

Halston

Roy Halston Frowick, known in fashion circles simply as Halston, opened his first hat business in Chicago in 1953. After the *Chicago Daily News* ran a brief story on his hats, his fame took off and he opened his own shop, the Boulevard Salon. In 1957 he moved to New York, first working for milliner Lilly Daché, followed by a head milliner position at department store Bergdorf Goodman. His big break came in 1961 when Jackie Kennedy wore one of his pillbox hats to her husband's presidential inauguration: his client list soon included the rich, beautiful and famous.

However, hats were falling out of favour in the Sixties as the young rejected conservative dress codes, and this seems to have influenced Halston's decision to move into womenswear. Backed by a Texas millionaire, he opened his first boutique on Madison Avenue in 1968. His clothes, like Pucci's in the previous decade, were characterised by comfort, clean lines and an understanding of the modern woman's needs. He told US *Vogue* he wanted to simplify the female wardrobe and do away with anything superfluous – clothes had to work. His modern creations in cashmere, chiffon and Ultrasuede – the fabric that would become his hallmark – quickly attracted an impressive list of celebrity fans including Anjelica Huston, Lauren Bacall, Elizabeth Taylor, Bianca Jagger and Liza Minnelli, who could not get enough of his sexy yet elegant pieces.

Launching his first ready-to-wear line in 1969 saw his popularity skyrocket and by the start of the Seventies Halston was a millionaire. The rise of disco in the first half of the decade only added to his popularity as Halston's mini and maxi dresses in stretchy materials allowed free movement of the body and were perfect for dancing. His soft, often draped (at times Grecian-inspired), relatively unconstructed separates and dresses became the unofficial Studio 54 uniform; his evening wear came in brighter colours, but for daywear he favoured pale pinks and shades of bone, tan and taupe. His fluid shirt dresses, strapless gowns, halter-neck jumpsuits, tops and dresses, caftans and liquid jersey separates were not just worn for going out: his disco styles significantly impacted on leisurewear, which during the decade took on board the comfort element and provided people with casual yet fashionable separates.

Throughout the decade Halston expanded his empire to include menswear, accessories, lingerie and even bedding. Like Pucci before him, in 1977 Halston was commissioned to design Braniff International Airways uniforms – a scheme the company christened Ultra-Touch. Halston's design ethos, shapes and colour palette perfectly captured the decade's mood.

Opposite *Beverly Johnson modelling a Halston maxi dress made of pastel-coloured vertical pieces of flowing chiffon jersey with a plunging neckline to the waist. The image captures why Halston's creations were perfect for dancing and favoured by the rich and famous at Studio 54.*

Ralph Lauren

Right *Ralph Lauren photographed in 1970.*

Opposite *Ralph Lauren (centre), along with staff members and models, in his 7th Avenue office, New York, November 1977. The staff and models' attire, in addition to the casual placement of polo clubs against the fire surround, sum up the RL look and brand perfectly. This mixture of old English landed gentry with the American Dream positioned RL as the aspirational attire of choice.*

Ralph Lauren (originally Ralph Lifshitz) was born into an immigrant family in the Bronx, New York. After studying business for two years – and after a brief stint in the army – he took a sales job at Brooks Brothers, where he learned about menswear. In the late Sixties, spotting a gap in the market, Lauren designed a range of men's ties and started selling them under the Polo brand in large department stores across the United States. Their success, based as much on their design as their clever branding, allowed Lauren to expand his range and soon a full menswear clothing line was added, which earned him a Coty Award in 1970.

This industry recognition encouraged him to release a womenswear range of tailored suits and blouses that borrowed heavily from men's tailoring and came in a wide variety of fabrics. His womenswear presented an imaginary, yet infinitely popular melange of modernity and English landed gentry styles. Like his male Polo brand, Lauren marketed his womenswear as the classic WASP style, successfully tapping into the aspirations of the American middle classes.

By 1971, Polo Ralph Lauren launched its first women's collection of apparel and the first stand-alone store opened in Beverly Hills, testifying to its phenomenal success. When, in 1974, Lauren was invited to design Robert Redford's costumes for *The Great Gatsby*, he immediately spotted the marketing opportunity and began offering suits that differed very little from his costumes, giving customers the opportunity to dress like Hollywood stars. It was

strangely fitting that he was chosen for *The Great Gatsby* as, like the story's main character, Lauren had big dreams of what luxury could be (and how the look didn't necessarily have to match the budget) and his own lines presented an updated version of Gatsby's aspirational lifestyle. Lauren was thus not a fashion innovator in the strict sense of the term – his designs were not cutting-edge, nor did they revolutionise fashion, but his business and branding sense certainly did.

From the outset of his career, Lauren used his prodigious retail knowledge to build his brand around an idealised preppy American image; he correctly translated the aspirational American dream into consumer goods by combining classic cuts, chic leisurewear and an American perception of British style. He was instrumental in creating the lifestyle brand, extending his range to childrenswear, fragrances and a home furnishings line that included wallpaper, towels, sheets, condiments and tableware, allowing his customers to live, eat and breathe Ralph Lauren.

His advertising was instrumental in his success and again marked him as a true business innovator; his understanding of American culture and the myths on which it was founded allowed him to set out updated versions of it in his campaigns (which often ran to six or eight pages, creating a immersive story that allowed customers to imagine themselves as part of the Lauren club). These ads have helped to define how the American Dream is visualised.

Kenzo

and opened Jungle Jap ('Jap' being the pejorative term for Japanese people – Kenzo reclaimed it and used it ironically). Here he sold loose casual clothes such as smocks, tent dresses, oversize dungarees and shirts, circular skirts and Peruvian knits, and he promoted a voluminous layered look. He also offered knitwear which, like Schiaparelli's, presented innovative designs in unexpected colour combinations.

Merging fun prints with an ethnic vibe, flowers (the house's signature) and textures to blend natural Japanese influences with Parisian culture, Kenzo created an East-meets-West aesthetic. His success was immediate and his eclectic designs embodied the Seventies youth's desire for individuality and difference.

Kenzo was very much part of the new Parisian group of emerging design talent (including the likes of Karl Lagerfeld, Sonia Rykiel, Jean Paul Gaultier and Jean-Charles de Castelbajac) that sought to bring luxury ready-to-wear to a wider and younger audience. Stylewise, Kenzo became known for his clashing colours and prints and his eclectic sources of inspiration, and he was one of the first to offer ethnic-chic ready-to-wear. His often-playful designs were hugely popular with celebrities and ordinary customers alike.

Kenzo is credited with creating (or popularising) many of the Seventies' key looks, such as oversized tunics, Mao collars, layering, oversized square jumpers, baggy trousers and shirts and the ethnic style. His idiosyncratic style has gone on to influence designers such as Romeo Gigli and Dries Van Noten as well as the Japanese designers of the Eighties, who may have rejected his colour palette in favour of black but who nevertheless continued his play with volume and his practice of applying Eastern cutting techniques to Western-style garments.

Kenzo Takada was born in Himeji, Japan to traditional innkeeper parents. After a brief stint studying literature he enrolled at Tokyo's Bunka fashion school, and within two years he was winning Japanese fashion awards. He joined the Sanai department store where he designed girls clothing, but soon he left Japan and moved to Paris in 1964 to pursue his high fashion dreams. Inspired by the space-age fashions of Paris, he began working as a freelance designer for couturiers and department stores.

In 1970 Kenzo opened his first shop, where he sold colourful clothes in a mix of bold prints. His aesthetic was as much down to necessity as personal vision: his limited budget meant he initially could only afford to buy vintage fabrics from flea markets, which as a result saw him mixing various prints in one garment. His clothes soon started attracting the attention of young, hip customers and within a year he moved premises

Opposite *Kenzo Takada.*

Left *Models on the Paris catwalk as part of Kenzo's 1972 prêt-à-porter Spring/ Summer collection. The signature style of Kenzo is the fusion of East and West. Here traditional Japanese footwear is paired with Thirties-style sportswear.*

The Prairie or Milkmaid Look

Seventies nostalgia styles took many forms and revisited a variety of historic periods. Few of these were more successful than what is known as the Milkmaid (UK) or Prairie (US) style, which saw adults and children alike adorned in highly romanticised late nineteenth-century inspired outfits.

In the UK, the style's most important promoter was Welsh designer Laura Ashley. Ashley had started printing headscarves with small Victorian calico designs in the Fifties, but it was in the late Sixties that she started offering complete outfits. Her Milkmaid look was no historic copy but rather a nostalgic, soft-focus concoction of far-off 'simpler' times seen through rose-tinted glasses; it was escapist, ultra-feminine and a touch conservative. It was also ultra-popular, and Ashley became a fashion sensation and a millionaire. While in the UK Ashley's designs were sold as 'English pastoral', in America they were marketed through the pioneer/early homesteaders myth.

The look's popularity owed much to the hit US television show *The Little House on the Prairie*, but it cannot simply be written off as a mere popular culture phenomenon. This rise of the pastoral look was most certainly an escape to past times that were easy to imagine as simpler and thus safer – especially given the economic upheaval that marked the second half of the decade. However, they can also be seen as a response to the growing discussions and worries about ecological issues. A mainstream engagement with eco-politics directly contributed to the decade's fashions through a revival of arts and crafts techniques, including patchwork, appliquéd, hand-knitted and crocheted garments, and through a promotion of styles worn by those perceived to have lived in a historic rural idyll.

White cotton Prairie/Milkmaid dress by Montreal designer Jean Christophe. These retro dresses drew from a host of historic sources including Empire styles, late eighteenth-century chemise dresses, early twentieth-century lingerie dresses and romantic pioneer myths.

Laura Ashley's Milkmaid clothes mixed Victorian patterns with Edwardian-inspired dress designs; her cotton midi and maxi dresses, smocks, pinafores and skirts often featured ruffled necklines or hems, leg-of-mutton sleeves, lace inserts or hems and petticoats that had a distinctly pastoral feel to them.

⊕ The most popular brand of Prairie dresses in the United States was produced by the San Francisco company Gunne Sax, who became synonymous with the look and who, like Ashley, offered endless variations of the style. Cheaper versions of these rustic fashions could also be purchased through the Sears Roebuck catalogue, which described them as 'reminiscent of early American settlers'.

⊕ At the high end of the market, Ralph Lauren presented slightly sexier versions of the look in 1978, offering denim skirts worn over lace petticoats and ditsy lace blouses.

Terrorist Chic

Terrorist Chic is the sartorial expression of flirtations with radical ideologies on the part of celebrities, socialites and the higher echelons of society – not because of any great belief in the causes they supported (including the IRA and Baader–Meinhoff/Red Army Faction), but fuelled by a postmodern desire to be confrontational and fashionably shocking.

Like the Prairie look, it was a response or a reaction to what was happening in society at large, but unlike the pastoral styles it did not try to shy away from reality by hiding in history, and instead faced the issues with bravado, aggression and at times bad taste, in the same way as Punk did.

Designers associated with the style, such as Mugler and Lagerfeld, made black leather stylish precisely because it evoked images of sadomasochistic sex, which was regarded as the last taboo. Pornographic movies like *Angelique in Black Leather* and art films such as *Maîtresse* (which was about a dominatrix, and featured fetish costumes in leather and rubber by Karl Lagerfeld) contributed to this deviant mystique. Fashion photography translated the mood into often highly fetishistic and brutal imagery; photographers Helmut Newton and Guy Bourdin epitomised this aesthetic development. Newton's work featured women wearing fetishistic outfits in highly charged sexual situations, while Bourdin's demonstrated a penchant for brutalised or seemingly dead female bodies.

The whole look was only worn by a minority, yet several of the items popularised by the style were adopted into mainstream fashion, which diluted and often disassociated them from their original meaning.

Pierre Cardin and models in the late Seventies. Terrorist Chic as an aesthetic was rarely worn as a full look, although certain designers presented it as such in their collection presentations. Mostly the look resided in details such as militaristic accentuated shoulders and stark tailoring.

● While the more extreme Terrorist Chic designs by Mugler were aimed at a niche audience, other designers offered more understated versions of the style. Daniel Hechter evoked a paramilitary ethos by using black berets to accessorise leather coats and tweed suits.

● The use of military tailoring was another significant feature and was evident in the popularity of items such as trench coats and berets at the more harmless and less explicit end of the Terrorist Chic spectrum.

Dark Glamour

Fashion in the Seventies saw many previous decades dusted off and given a new sartorial airing. On the more conservative end of the spectrum, Prairie or Milkmaid styles ruled; however, at the other end reworkings of glamorous Thirties fashions were equally popular and available to those who did not wish to pursue the look of innocence. Golden-Age Hollywood fashions had raised eyebrows and pulses first time round, and their Seventies reincarnation often managed to replicate this effect by giving the look a darker, more decadent twist.

London fashion label Biba was at the forefront of the Thirties fashion revival, and did not merely copy the past but instead exaggerated it through subtle changes in materials, colour palette and cut: Biba models and customers looked like the sexy twin sisters of their Thirties counterparts, all heavily made-up eyes and lips.

Biba's revivalist character was not limited to their clothes; their flagship store on Kensington High Street (housed in the famous Thirties department store Derry & Toms) had been immaculately restored to its former Art Deco glory inside and out. The dark, barely lit interior of black lacquered wood, mirrored fittings and plush dark-brown patterned upholstery was a combination of a Thirties boudoir and an opium den, oozing with the seductive glamour of days gone by. The lingerie and upmarket womenswear departments were littered with chaises longues upholstered in leopard print, vases filled with ostrich and peacock feathers (directly copied from *Dinner at Eight*), fringed and beaded lights and large Art Deco mirrors.

—— Twiggy in a faux-leopard maxi coat from Biba, which was one of the pioneers of a darker retro-chic. The store and its clothes were reminiscent of Hollywood's Golden Age but added a louche twist; the whole concept was Busby Berkeley meets Mata Hari.

● The Thirties revival was not limited to London: on the Parisian catwalks interwar influences could easily be discerned in collections by the likes of Balmain, Mugler and Cardin; even Halston's draped or clinging maxi fashions often had a Thirties feel to them.

1980s

If the Seventies were the 'Me' decade – a phrase the American writer Tom Wolfe used to define the individualistic tendencies of the time – the Eighties are surely best described as the 'Gimme' decade. The economic changes introduced at the start of the decade by Prime Minister Margaret Thatcher in the UK, and President Ronald Reagan in the USA, brought about a vast increase of wealth and disposable income for those in the upper-income strata, and this resulted in a boom of luxury consumerism and the glorification of the designer brand.

Conspicuous consumption of ready-to-wear designer brands, ostentatious Haute Couture fashions and aggressive logo culture (allowing their followers to literally wear their pay cheques on their chests – or belts and bags as in Moschino's case), resulted in the decade being typified as an era of greed and excess in the world of fashion.

This excess found expression in many different guises: from the indulgent Haute Couture creations of French designer Christian Lacroix to the expensive but understated work suits by Armani, and from the exaggerated shoulders on womenswear to the bright colours and lurid prints that characterised the middle years of the decade. Excess could reside in the design, the price tag, or both.

Dress for Success

The Dress for Success style that had emerged in the Seventies dominated Eighties fashion, albeit with some marked changes. The trouser suit was mostly abandoned, and instead short skirts were now teamed with jackets that had padded shoulders and presented a far more masculine, at times near-militaristic look. These broad padded shoulders have often been interpreted as women merely adopting a masculine silhouette to assert themselves as equals in the

Left *Evening dress of heavily embroidered red velvet corset, black dotted transparent gauze sleeves and grey and pink gauze full skirt. Lacroix's excessive and fantastical couture designs had been a hit since the mid-Eighties; after the financial crash, however, many considered them to be in bad taste.*

workplace, and this assumption is anchored by the look being referred to both at the time and retrospectively as Power Dressing. It is true that this look was particularly popular with working women, and that the Eighties saw an increase of employment opportunities for women in more powerful and executive roles, but to assume they were merely copying men, either due to a lack of imagination or simply to emulate them, removes women's agency and ignores the short skirts worn with these jackets. Instead, one needs to accept that different women had different, often multiple, reasons for adopting the trend.

1980s

Postmodern Fashion

The master of extravagant Eighties evening wear was Christian Lacroix. Initially designing for the House of Patou, Lacroix founded his own maison in 1987. His luxurious but witty fantasy fashions in a riot of colours, embellishments and trims graced the pages of magazines worldwide. Indebted to Charles James, Lacroix's creations tended to have rather simple but exquisitely moulded top halves and extravagant skirts that came in a variety of shapes. He often presented a reinterpretation of historic silhouettes, such as his structured upside-down lily silhouette, his nod to Fifties Balmain and James (whose famous Swan, Cloverleaf and Butterfly gowns had already played with history in their time) and his most famous 'invention', the pouf

skirt or dress, which resembled a short version of an eighteenth-century mantua with extra draping and bows thrown in for good measure. Lacroix's designs, like those of so many during the Eighties, played with the past, knowingly and humorously interpreting history. This was postmodern fashion.

Karl Lagerfeld, who had moved from Chloé to Chanel in 1982, also confronted history, albeit in a more introspective manner. Charged with bringing Maison Chanel's designs up to date without losing the core style of the brand and its founder, he set about deconstructing the iconic Chanel looks. The classic tweed jacket was shortened and versions were produced in denim, towelling fabric and stretchy man-made materials. This move might have put off Chanel's traditional customers,

but it introduced the style to a young and hip generation. The classic Chanel knee-length skirt went in one of two directions: it was either dropped right to the ankles, or exposed most of the thigh. Even the understated chic of Chanel's costume jewellery did not escape his reworking: the 'new' Chanel suit was accessorised with necklaces and belts of oversized fake pearls, gold and leather chains and bejewelled interlocking 'C's, the house's logo. He neither copied nor dismissed Chanel's original designs but instead, like Lacroix, offered his own clever and witty version of the past.

New Radicals

The excess and humour that characterised postmodern Haute-Couture designs was best represented in ready-to-wear by France's enfant terrible, Jean Paul Gaultier, who did not only play with history but, more shockingly, also played with gender stereotypes in his collections. He sent men down the catwalk in skirts, and women in conical corset dresses that mocked their historic originals through exaggeration, questioning gender, sex and fetishism in a humorous and fun way.

However, he was far from being the only one to experiment sartorially with sex and fetishism. While in London Vivienne Westwood showed corsets and 'mini-crinis' (short bell-shaped skirts with collapsible hoops inspired by nineteenth-century crinolines), in Paris the Tunisian-born Azzedine Alaïa proposed ultra-feminine body-hugging silhouettes in stretchy materials whose seams emphasised a woman's curves. His dresses, jumpsuits, bodysuits and leggings were widely copied and these clinging fashions trickled down onto the high street with ease and success.

Opposite *Karl Lagerfeld suits, 1986. Aside from work at Chanel, Lagerfeld designed his own lines. These tailored redingotes (a French word borrowed from the English 'riding coat') nipped at the waist and belted with a buckle in his trademark fan shape, present a more modern, daring take on the traditional Power suit.*

Above *Jean Paul Gaultier's 1985 collection of cone bras and dresses in shirred velvet, following his men-in-skirts controversy of the previous year, confirmed JPG as the enfant terrible of fashion.*

Although sexualised, Alaïa's women were not mere passive objects of male fantasy: their sexuality was assertive and in line with the new female empowerment seen in the professional sphere. French designer Thierry Mugler's women went a step further, and their sexuality could only be defined as aggressive. Mugler presented a combination of the fetish–bodycon (body-conscious) trend and the power-dressing look. His curve-glorifying dresses worn with broad-shouldered jackets featured overt fetishistic references such as corsets, corset belts and lacing, and were accessorised with leather opera gloves and boots. His love for metallic fabrics that were often layered to resemble armour gave his creations an otherworldly feel and his women resembled alien warrior dominatrixes.

This rise of fetish underwear-as-outerwear fashion was in many ways an evolution of the Seventies Terrorist Chic look, mixed in with glamorised Punk elements. But while this may explain the style, its popularity in the opening decades of the 1980s can be ascribed to a disastrous external development: the AIDS epidemic. The psychoanalytical definition of a fetish as an inanimate object that becomes a substitute for the sexual act contextualises the rise in popularity of these fetish fashions: at a time when sex became a deadly serious matter, the shifting of sexual interest from the body to the outfit made perfect sense.

Going Logo

While sartorial experimentation and social antagonisms explain the fetish aspect of certain bodycon styles, they do not necessarily account for the popularity of other skintight clothing. Leggings, tapered trousers (often with stirrups) and skinny jeans defined the era's leisurewear, and their popularity owes much to the decade's body-consciousness and accompanying workout craze.

The designer-denim craze that had started in the second half of the Seventies grew to epic proportions in the 'Age of Acquisition'. Calvin Klein's were the jeans to be seen in. The American designer rejected the ostentation of Chanel and Lacroix and publicly declared his disdain for fussy fashion. Instead, he presented understated looks.

This sartorial minimalism became a popular alternative to the conspicuous excess of Paris and was promoted by several other American and German designers including Jil Sander (dubbed by the press as the 'queen of less'), Donna Karan (who started her label in 1984 and whose Essential line included just seven pieces which could be mixed and matched) and Anne Klein (a label that, like Karan – who was its designer until the opening of her own house – offered a modular wardrobe of classics and essentials). Their approach to fashion foregrounded comfort, and while not obviously excessive in terms of design or decoration, its luxury

Opposite Thierry Mugler, ready-to-wear, Autumn/Winter 1984, Paris. Mugler's designs often featured corsets and breastplates, which the press described as fetishist. Undoubtedly an element of fetish wear was present, but uniform and militarist dress was an equally important inspiration, as seen in this silhouette: the leather vest top resembles a centurion cuirass.

Right The Calvin Klein CK logo, designed by Welsh designer Jeffrey Banks in the early 1970s, is one of the world's most recognisable fashion logos, second only to the Chanel interlocking CC. Grasping people's desire for conspicuous consumption and display Calvin Klein often applied the logo to garments in prominent places – back pockets on jeans, the front of handbags and across the chest on T-shirts.

resided in the superior fabrics (cashmere, silk and high-quality wool) used in their more expensive lines. Most also offered cheaper ranges, thereby both fuelling and responding to the trickled-down desire for the designer gear flaunted by the rich.

One of the cheapest items became another Eighties classic: the designer T-shirt. While some, like Sander, only sold plain, non-branded T-shirts, many others sold T-shirts and polo shirts with their logos or brand names emblazoned on the chest, the most famous and successful of these being Ralph Lauren, whose polo-player logo became near-universally recognisable.

Heavily branded goods were not just limited to T-shirts – their popularity proved so big that soon whole (often cheaper) ranges of garments that clearly spelled out the brand or creator's name flooded the market. The design of these was often basic and they mostly included casual items such as sweatshirts and vest tops; accessories such as bags, baseball caps and watches; and, of course, underwear, which was central to Calvin Klein's success. The basic design of these items highlighted the start of a shift towards dematerialisation and a consumption of brands rather than goods, where the emphasis was on the sign value, not the material value of objects.

Fashion Fusion

While the minimal look grew in popularity as the decade wore on, it by no means went unchallenged. Designers such as Italian Romeo Gigli and Kenzo Takada from Japan proposed alternatives to both the minimal and the bodycon styles through their soft and often layered romantic fashions, which presented a more luxurious and polished version of the New Romantics' looks, fashionable in the clubs of London (these had also inspired Vivienne Westwood's Pirate collection). Their mix of historicism and exoticism led to the designers being dubbed 'Neo-Orientalists', but unlike their historic predecessors (Poiret et al.) their Orientalism revolved more around experimentation with cut and volume than theatrical detail.

This play with shape and volume was taken to new conceptual heights by Japanese designers Issey Miyake, Yohji Yamamoto and Rei Kawakubo (founder of Comme des Garçons). Each presented a new form of cultural hybridity that fused Eastern traditional garment-making techniques with modern Western fabrics and sensibilities. The kimono was endlessly reinterpreted by Miyake, whose creations explored the void between body and garment; Yamamoto's folded and pleated garments referenced traditional Eastern dress; and Kawakubo's seemingly unfinished, dishevelled or ripped garments (which the press pejoratively dubbed 'the aesthetics of poverty') rejected the tailored and manipulated Western shape and instead created clothing that could simply be wrapped around the body and shaped by the wearer. All were evidence of an understanding of, and a respect for, textiles in their creations (in opposition to the dematerialisation of mass-produced designer ready-to-wear) and their new shapes were equally, if not more, radical in regard to gender-bending and subversion than those suggested by Western designers.

Style Deconstructed

These new alternative aesthetics borrowed ideas from contemporary conceptual art and successfully applied them to design; in so doing, they questioned the very essence of fashion. No designer embodied this new critical approach better than Martin Margiela, who first showed in 1988 and immediately became the king of deconstruction. Not only did he 'deconstruct' actual garments, reworking them to expose the 'making' process that is essentially invisible in fashion (its exposure reminds us that fashion is artificial and a construct, and limits its totemic powers), his designs also deconstructed the very nature of luxury fashion through his use of recycled, second-hand and deliberately cheap materials such as plastic bags and broken plates. Thus, Margiela posed the question whether luxury is material-bound or culturally created and dictated by fashion.

Eighties (like Seventies) fashion thus remained linked to the past through its appropriation of history. The decade's investigation and deconstruction of history not only led to the introduction of new fashionable shapes and styles but, more importantly, these in turn allowed the questioning, and at times the subversion, of gender stereotypes and the very nature of fashion itself.

Above *Issey Miyake, ready-to-wear, Autumn/ Winter 1985, Paris. In the Eighties Miyake began experimenting with heat-press pleating techniques (as seen on this ensemble), which led to the establishment in 1989 of his Pleats Please line: polyester jersey garments that were pleated after construction. His pleated designs echo Fortuny's early twentieth-century designs.*

Christian Lacroix

Above *Lacroix, Haute Couture, Autumn/ Winter 1987, Paris. The wedding dress applies Lacroix's pouf to what is essentially a hobble skirt design. As in so many of his creations history is updated in an innovative idiosyncratic manner.*

Christian Lacroix was born in Arles in the south of France, and from a young age showed a keen interest in historical costume. His began his career as a fashion assistant at Hermès; from there he moved to Guy Paulin where he worked as an assistant in accessories, and after a stint at a fashion house in Tokyo he became head designer at the couture house Patou in 1981. While in the first few years he designed collections inspired by what Jean Patou had produced in his heyday, over time Lacroix started to develop what would become his signature style, one marked by opulence and extravagance.

By 1984 his creations were attracting a younger, hipper audience to Patou, but it was his 1985 collection in luxurious fabrics, in rich Mediterranean colours inspired by his childhood, that really put him in the limelight and turned him into a fashion superstar.

His 1986 collection introduced both the bubble and the pouf dress, which became instant fashion hits and were widely copied by ready-to-wear companies. His knowledge of historic costume shone through his collections, which featured bustles, leg-of-mutton sleeves and pannier skirts. But it was his innovative and daring use of colour and his lavish embellishments that really captured the decade's spirit of excess. He was credited with making Haute Couture fun again by infusing it with a fantasy and exuberance not seen since the evening gowns of the Fifties.

While his couture creations had made him the toast of the fashion world, Lacroix, acutely aware of the influence his couture designs were having on the mass market, was eager to design ready-to-wear. However, Maison Patou would not allow this, which led him, in 1987, to open his own couture house and add a ready-to-wear collection to his output. His first collection under his own name moved away from the pouf-like silhouettes he had shown in previous seasons and instead focused on even more intricate and excessive embellishments and trimmings of lace, jewels and fur. His knowing references to historic costume and fashion greats, combined with his vibrant prints and colour combinations, and his frivolous and witty approach to design, made him the most famous designer of the Eighties.

In 1988 he presented his first ready-to-wear collection, which was inspired by his Haute Couture offerings but used prints as a substitute for the lavish embroideries. A second line was added soon after to increase the company's profitability (Haute Couture acted as a shop window for the brand but mostly operated at a loss), as were accessories and jewellery.

Towards the end of the decade, when the economic and political climate started changing, the mainstream press started to turn against Lacroix, criticising his opulence as vulgar after the 1987 stock market crash and out of touch with what working women wore. Nevertheless, Lacroix continued to be influential into the early Nineties.

Left *Lacroix, ready-to-wear, Spring/Summer 1989. While at Patou Lacroix wanted to design ready-to-wear alongside his Haute Couture collections but contractually he was prevented from doing so. Once he set up under his own name he introduced a more affordable off-the-peg line that bore his colourful hallmark style. Here he pays tribute to his Provençal roots through his updating of traditional textile patterns.*

Thierry Mugler

Thierry Mugler, christened 'the prophet of futurism' by the fashion press, was born in Strasbourg, where he began his career as a professional dancer before moving to Paris in 1968. Here he started working as a window dresser while simultaneously freelancing for couturiers. He designed his womenswear collections in the early Seventies with the help of Azzedine Alaïa; the two would collaborate until the end of the decade.

In 1974 he started designing under his own name and his collections were an immediate success with more cutting-edge buyers. While the rest of the world was still wearing hippy-chic flowing garments, Mugler presented a collection that sculpted the body and oozed sexuality. Combined with his love for military uniform and dominating colours, which he incorporated in many of his silhouettes, his aggressive style, with overtly fetishistic overtones, presented a whole new idea of femininity that would become hugely influential in the Eighties.

Mugler was one of the first designers to present the power-dressing look, paving the way for Jean Paul Gaultier, Claude Montana and his former collaborator, Alaïa. His style of power dressing combined extremely wide shoulders, nipped waists (achieved through wide leather or PVC belts, moulded corsets, tailored jackets or breastplates) and hip-hugging skirts, bodysuits and trousers, often with high waists. The woman he presented was all-powerful, aggressive and at times a near-alien femme fatale (this same type of woman is clearly visible in Alexander McQueen's early collections). Mugler's strong, angular looks were often adorned with dramatic, intimidating details such as cut-outs, pointed angles on collars, hems and sleeves, or flame embellishments in coloured PVC, leather or crystals. The look was finished off with devil features such as hair gel-slicked into horns.

His flair for theatrics led Mugler to stage his first supershow in 1984 to celebrate his first ten years in fashion. The extravaganza, which flirted with the liturgy, sexuality and the divine, was attended by over 6,000 people.

While the fashion-forward press and devoted customers adored Mugler, many others opposed his vision of femininity, accusing him of hyper-sexualisation at best and misogyny at worst. His provocative outspokenness did not help and, in real life just as in his fashion designs, Mugler was out to shock, releasing books in praise of fetishism and citing Nazi film director Leni Riefenstahl as the ideal woman.

Above *Thierry Mugler (centre), posing with Lady Miss Kier and Towa Tei from the pop group Deee-Lite at a Paris fashion week party in the Eighties.*

Opposite *Thierry Mugler, Autumn/Winter 1984, Paris. Mugler's designs often included interesting fabric combinations – here fur and metallic-coated leather. Models were often styled as predatory aliens and the sexual but strong femininity he put forward is similar to that found in McQueen's work of the Nineties.*

Yohji Yamamoto

After completing his law degree in Tokyo in 1966, Yohji Yamamoto enrolled at the Bunka fashion college, graduating in 1969. He launched his Y-line in 1977 and debuted in Paris in 1981. This womenswear collection featured black and dark grey oversized jackets, coats, maxi skirts and sack dresses that enveloped the models' bodies. While Kenzo Takada had introduced a fashion for oversized garments in the previous decades, Yamamoto's colour blocking (predominantly grey, blue, white and red in his first collection, later foregrounding black) and innovative masculine cutting gave these garments a wholly different more understated and intellectual feel.

Yamamoto's clothes were in direct opposition to the output of the 'kings of cling' and instead of accentuating or exaggerating the female body he de-emphasised it through his cutting and layering. In so doing he not only ignored current trends (which has been a hallmark of his career) but actively questioned gender. His oversized, seemingly unfinished garments in unusual

or unexpected fabrics such as neoprene, also challenged accepted notions of fashion and luxury.

His designs quickly marked him out as a master cutter, tailor and draper and comparisons to Madeleine Vionnet were aplenty. His designs became increasingly sculptural (in particular in his felt pieces) yet remained wearable through his creation of space between the body and the fabric; comfort was central to his aesthetic. He soon became labelled as the anti-fashion designer, drawing inspiration from traditional Japanese costume, in particular the kimono, and peasant dress, favouring asymmetry to the neatness and fluid cuts of the early Eighties.

Central to his work were textiles – fabric, he said, was everything – and he often employed traditional Japanese craftsmen to make his fabrics meet his specific orders; he layered various fabrics and played with contrasting texture instead of colour, black becoming his signature. His lack of colour allowed his pattern cutting to take centre stage and he quickly gained faithful followers who saw his clothes, and those of the other two Japanese designers in Paris, Rei Kawakubo and Issey Miyake, as art and as a viable alternative to the more form-fitting fashions of the decade.

In 1984, he introduced a menswear collection that in terms of design and cut was very similar to his womenswear lines, and he often stated in interviews that when he started designing clothes he wanted women to wear men's clothes. Yamamoto went on to win numerous awards in the Eighties and Nineties and his influence can be seen in the Belgian designers who emerged in the late Eighties and the minimalist lines of Jil Sander and Helmut Lang of the early Nineties.

Above *Master tailor Yohji Yamamoto.*

Opposite *Late Eighties Yamamoto Z-shaped belted jacket in navy blue gabardine and knife-pleated midi skirt worn with his crushed leather gauntlet gloves.*

The Pouf Skirt

While the Eighties, with its variety of styles and looks, did not have one defining style, it did have certain defining characteristics, and 'pouffiness' – a preference for puffball-like shapes – was one of them.

Parisian and American designers offered glamorous evening dresses with a host of historic-style puffed or gathered sleeves, but it was London designers such as Zandra Rhodes and Vivienne Westwood who offered a more avant-garde and interesting play with volume in their creations. Their work was often the perfect mediation between high fashion and the subcultural styles of the capital, in particular New Romanticism. The New Romantics had appeared in the late Seventies and their culture peaked around 1981 (incidentally the height of puffed sleeves). Their fashions were a fantastical mix of reimagined historical styles, including Elizabethan, Victorian and Thirties glamour looks, and were often characterised by volume play. These luxurious pouf-like styles seen on the global catwalks were thus a postmodern bubble of fashion that were evidence of the increasing importance of youth and subcultural styles and their influence on mainstream high fashion.

The vogue for pouffiness had waned by the closing years of the decade, in part due to its conspicuous excess being considered vulgar at a time of deepening economic divides, but also owing to the increased popularity of form-fitting fashions championed by Parisian and Italian designers.

Christian Lacroix showed a stylised Spanish ensemble of a Castilian hat, a black, richly embroidered matador jacket and a balloon or pouf dress as part of his Haute Couture collection, Paris, 1987. The outfit exemplifies Lacroix's knowledge of historic and regional dress and his ability to transform that knowledge into high fashion.

⊕ Sleeves and shoulders were artificially enhanced through either nineteenth-century-style leg-of-mutton sleeves (most famously witnessed on Princess Diana's 1981 wedding dress designed by Elizabeth and David Emanuel) or excessive Thirties-style ruffles (often seen on the cast members of the hit TV show *Dynasty*).

⊕ Lacroix for the house of Patou debuted his bouffant (or pouf or bubble) evening skirt, a short, full, puffy garment derived from the Fifties bubble skirt but which, unlike its historic predecessor, was short and frothy, seemingly made of fabric meringues. The style became an immediate hit and the next collections each side of the Atlantic saw designers including their own versions of the bouffant. The most notable of these were Bill Blass's swinging skirts with petticoats and Karl Lagerfeld for Chanel's ruffled petticoats and big skirts.

The Power Suit

The Power Suit was a conservative two-piece skirt suit in dark 'serious' colours and natural fabrics, worn with a modest high-necked blouse, plain pumps and a briefcase. At the fashion show of Louis Feraud in the department store KaDeWe Berlin in 1985 models wore day and evening versions of the Power suit, illustrating its popularity and acceptance as appropriate womenswear in and outside of the office.

Jacket shoulders were accentuated with pads that in their more excessive incarnations looked almost militaristic, often set off by a nipped waist. Adverts featured terms such as 'strongly defined', 'broader', 'masculine', 'bigger' shoulders. To 'feminise' the look the jacket was teamed with a narrow skirt and a bow or ruffled blouse.

⊕ Italian designers, Giorgio Armani in particular, had a significant impact on suit design, and indeed his looser, less constructed looks (which did away with stiff inner linings and paddings) offered a sleek alternative to the more traditional Power Suit.

No other word more clearly defines the Eighties than 'power', and no other look is more associated with it than power dressing.

After the phenomenal success of John Molloy's *Dress for Success* (1975) and *The Women's Dress for Success Book* (1977), which had set out dress codes for the corporate world, women in the Eighties began to adopt the Success or Power Suit, in pursuit of professional equality with men. This uniform look had a nearly immediate and profound impact on the fashion industry, and of the top ten American suit producers for men in the Seventies, seven added women's lines.

By the start of the Eighties, the diversity of suits on the market suggested that women wanted to be taken seriously but did not want or need to be liberated from fashion altogether. It seemed that women (and men, albeit for different reasons) preferred softer, less dreary and conservative silhouettes in lighter and brighter colours, and alongside the matching suit simple pieces such as dresses, blazers and cardigans were promoted as appropriate for middle and upper management.

However, while separates became popular, the tailored jacket (either as part of a matching suit or teamed with a skirt or, less frequently, trousers) reigned as the key 'power' fashion piece for business.

Black

The Eighties is most remembered for its vivid colour palette; while there is no denying that colour was omnipresent in daywear, it is often forgotten that black also returned as a key feature of the fashionable wardrobe.

The trend for designer jeans reached a peak in the Eighties, with the most desirable brands making fortunes off standardised mass-produced garments that featured logos to alert others of its origins, and that were aggressively marketed through attention-grabbing advertising campaigns.

⊕ Black items, including leggings, jackets, dresses and blouses were popular, although often teamed with brighter-coloured items or accessories; the top to toe in black was, for now, mostly reserved for the catwalk and the new 'style tribes' such as goths and pervs but the colour would go mainstream in the following decade.

One of the most persistent fashion myths concerns the colour black. It is commonly believed that it has been the colour of choice since the Twenties but while it has never quite disappeared from women's wardrobes its popularity ebbed and flowed from decade to decade. Throughout the Sixties and Seventies black pieces could be found in most Haute Couture collections and ready-to-wear, but more colourful palettes were predominant and indeed favoured by designers and their customers. In the Eighties, however, black made an important comeback for several reasons.

The rise of professional office wear for women in the mid-Seventies favoured more severe colours so as not to appear frivolous or too feminine; greys, browns, dark blues – black did feature but was not yet predominant. In the Eighties the popularity of black women's suits grew year on year. Black had been the colour of labour and industry for men since the early nineteenth century as it was inextricably bound up with the Industrial Revolution; it was hence considered appropriate work wear for women in the Twenties, and saw a revival every time significant advances were made for women in the workplace. The advances of second-wave feminism meant the late Seventies and Eighties saw an increasing number of women in managerial positions, and thus the resurgence of black can be explained as part of a wider pattern.

This was, though, not the only factor. Its use by the new breed of conceptual designers positioned black as the 'anti-fashion' fashion colour of choice. Miyake's, Kawakubo's and Yamamoto's extensive use of it in their collections saw it loaded with a host of associations and meanings that drew on the colour's history. Their artistic creations evoked black's Left-Bank intellectualism and the rebellious and bohemian spirit of the beats, rockers and punks. The Eighties saw black being cast as the colour of the avant-garde and the serious businesswoman alike.

1990s

In many ways, Nineties fashion was the culmination of the triumph of personal choice over the dictatorship of designers seen in the Seventies, combined with the postmodern fragmentation of looks into style tribes seen in the Eighties.

If the Eighties had many key looks, the Nineties had none, as their lifespan was often brief, and different looks defined different concurrent style groups.

Be the Brand

Through extensive market research and aggressive branding, fashion labels connected with and directly shaped their customers. They did not try to appeal to all but instead focused on fostering and extending their loyal clientele with aspirational advertising campaigns.

The brands one was loyal to sold a clearly defined lifestyle and identity that could be bought into; the extension of diffusion and lifestyle lines exemplified this. For example, Ralph Lauren not only offered men's, women's and children's lines but also perfumes and homewares including bathrobes, paint and wallpaper; in the closing year of the decade, Lauren opened his first restaurant and his fans could now literally live, breathe and eat the brand.

This lifestyle promotion resulted in brand loyalty as one picked the wish images that one aspired to and rejected others. The aspirational lifestyles communicated in advertising increasingly guided consumption over a consideration of design, which is why unimaginative products such as the Ralph Lauren polo shirt were so popular: not merely a polo shirt, but the representation of the American Dream. This meant a move into equating a brand's name with values that went beyond luxury or good design: consumer goods – however standardised – symbolised an identity that

Above *Destiny's Child promoting the Hilfiger brand in 1998. Throughout the Nineties many brands tried to associate themselves with black music culture in a bid to (cynically) enhance their street credibility; none did so more successfully than Tommy Hilfiger, who applied his trademark red, blue and white (all-American) logo to streetwear baggy jeans, boxer shorts, boob tubes and bomber jackets.*

could be chosen and acquired: the 'intellectual/artistic professional' (Jil Sander, Margiela, Helmut Lang, Prada), the 'edgy, streetwise rebel' (Anna Sui, Perry Ellis, Katharine Hamnett, Miu Miu), the 'sophisticated sex kitten' (Gucci, Iceberg, Versace), the 'wholesome and well-heeled affluent American' (Ralph Lauren, Tommy Hilfiger), and the 'ostentatious Mediterranean luxuriant' (Roberto Cavalli, Dolce & Gabbana, Blumarine), to name but a few. The carefully staged promotional material, which gave the impression of personal choice and identity while selling mass-produced, standardised products, created the illusion of individuality. This arguably became the most powerful selling tool of the decade.

Above *Naomi Campbell, pictured in 1997. Campbell was one of the few supermodels who managed to have a career after the Versace model mania of the early Nineties that was equally if not more successful than the one she had enjoyed as part of the supermodel pack.*

The Birth of the Supermodel

The rise in importance of advertising was accompanied by the growing importance and celebrity status of fashion models. This movement had started in the late Eighties, but only once Versace sent Naomi Campbell, Cindy Crawford, Christy Turlington and Linda Evangelista down the catwalk in 1991 did we witness the birth of the supermodel. These women's ability to sell products and change fashions (including hair and make-up fashions) was phenomenal and their glamorous lives and celebrity status only served to lend further 'sign value' to the clothes they modelled and the brands whose campaigns they fronted.

A fifth model who caught the press's attention was Kate Moss, who in 1992 starred with Mark Wahlberg in a Calvin Klein underwear campaign. A year later she became the face of Klein's Obsession fragrance and the adverts in which she posed naked catapulted her from relative obscurity into the global headlines. Her thinness compared to the Eighties 'Glamazonian' models, combined with her innocent teenage looks, elicited accusations of exploitation, anorexia and most famously 'Heroin Chic', a look typified by her pale skin, waifish figure and dark circles under the eyes. Despite the controversy (or because of it), sales of Calvin Klein fragrances, jeans and underwear boomed.

Opposite *Anna Sui, Spring 1993. The grunge-lux trend made a brief appearance in high fashion but was quickly dropped due to a lack of commercial success. Young people who were interested in the music or the look had cheaper options and older clients refused to pay high-end prices for often 'shabby' or cheap-looking pieces.*

From Grunge to the Gap

Aside from clever marketing, the Heroin Chic look has often been positioned as a reaction against the high glamour and greed of the Eighties – indeed, many popular looks and trends of the Nineties are framed as reactionary. The vogue for luxury Grunge fashion is one such example.

In the early Nineties, Grunge (a style of music that emerged in the mid-Eighties, often associated with Seattle bands such as Soundgarden, Alice in Chains and, most famously, Nirvana) saw its cheap, vernacular styles bubble up into the mainstream. Luxury versions of checked flannel shirts, floral dresses and combat boots were seen on the catwalk and featured in mainstream fashion magazines. *Vogue*'s 1992 Steven Meisel editorial 'Grunge and Glory' features pieces by Ralph Lauren and an $840 Calvin Klein dress, along with advice on how to layer. On the catwalks, American designer Anna Sui offered striped maxi dresses and matching beanies, and at US fashion house Perry Ellis (designed by Marc Jacobs) holed jumpers, silk slip dresses and flannel maxi shirts were the order of the day. The fashion press turned against Grunge chic as quickly as they had adopted it, however, as they realised people were not going to spend large amounts of money to look like scruffy teenagers; Marc Jacobs was dropped by Ellis and production of his collection was stopped.

Another popular (if not *the* most popular) style of the decade also fits into the anti-Eighties glamour bracket: minimalism. Started in the late Eighties, minimalism dominated both luxury and high-street fashion of the Nineties. Seen as a reaction against the likes of Lacroix, German designer Jil Sander and American Donna Karan continued to produce understated, wearable and comfortable clothes, often with a masculine touch, in muted colours. Austrian Helmut Lang and Prada (although the latter offered more feminine styles) also rode the wave of less ostentatious design by offering key pieces or 'basics'; however, the impeccably cut and tailored clothes in luxurious materials that came with high price tags were anything but basic. At the less expensive end of the fashion spectrum, and leaning more towards a relaxed and casual look, were brands such as Calvin Klein Jeans, CK Sportswear and the Gap, which offered 'real clothes' in the form of basic separates. It has been suggested that the look's success was down to people wanting to blend in with what they perceived as an increasingly fast-paced and aggressive urban society. But comfort also played a significant role; it was, after all, in the Nineties that the jeans and T-shirt combo became a global look.

1990s

Above *Gianni Versace with supermodels Naomi Campbell, Carla Bruni, Karen Mulder and Christy Turlington at the Versace Haute Couture fashion show Spring/Summer 1992. The inclusion of all of the day's most famous models made Versace's shows a true press frenzy and turned the brand into a household name.*

More Cultural Commodification

Many proclaimed this triumph of minimalism as the end of high glamour, yet by 1994 the catwalks and magazines once again heralded its return, this time in the shape of what certain parts of the press pejoratively termed the 'Power Slut'. Versace, Karl Lagerfeld for Chanel and the newly appointed Tom Ford at Gucci all presented their own versions. While the former two presented tailored suits with short skirts in candy-floss colours, Ford made his name at Gucci with his sleek and ultra-sexy evening dresses worn with spiked heels and lashings of red lipstick – this was not a reaction against Eighties power dressing and glamour, it was simply an updated version of it.

Another element of the previous decade's styles that resurfaced was that of appropriation, not only of the past but also of non-Western cultures. John Galliano's 1995 collection presented a mixture of late-Forties New Look suits, Victorian bustled skirts and corset blouses, a hobble skirt and Jacques Fath-inspired evening gowns.

Gucci borrowed from 1960s Mod culture for their 1995 collection and presented figure-hugging boot-cut velvet or satin trousers teamed with satin shirts in rich shades of blue and green that were either unbuttoned to reveal the bra worn underneath, or were simply worn without one.

Vivienne Westwood went further back into history and throughout the Nineties presented collections that referenced eighteenth-century French court fashions, early nineteenth-century Regency dresses and Victorian bustles and corsets with a tongue-in-cheek, sexy twist. Versace referenced the past in its print designs, but rarely ventured into history for its silhouettes: bomber jackets, silk shirts, dresses, leggings and blouses featured multicoloured and gold Baroque prints.

Influences from non-Western cultures were also a recurring feature, particularly in the Haute Couture collections by Galliano (first for Givenchy and later for Dior) in the latter half of the decade: African tribal beading, Native American featherwork, Eastern European and Russian embroidery, Mexican quilting all made an appearance but were never just reproductions – Galliano interpreted them in innovative ways and combined them with historical styles to create novelty.

This did not leave them immune from criticism; in particular, Galliano's frivolous use of Native American headdresses was not well received in all quarters. Jean Paul Gaultier had also run into trouble with his 1993 collection inspired by Hasidic Jews, which saw women dressed in long black coats and *shtreimels* (traditional Hasidic fur hats worn only by married men). None of these cultural/religious appropriations, though, caused controversy comparable to Chanel's 1994 catwalk presentation, which featured several dresses with verses from the Quran embroidered on the bodices, and which saw Lagerfeld

and Chanel forced to issue official apologies to the Muslim community worldwide.

While the press covered all these incidents, the debate about cultural appropriation in the Nineties very much focused on the use of black street styles by white designers. Owing to music's central role in youth culture, and because of the importance of African American artists in the Eighties and Nineties, black street style was one of the most important influences on clothing (especially for young people) throughout the decade. Chanel's 1991 Hip Hop collection saw its classic suit accessorised with chunky gold chains and big earrings, and even executed in quilted leather. Versace produced upmarket bomber jackets teamed with chunky gold jewellery. The biggest appropriator of the decade, however, had to be American designer Tommy Hilfiger, whose entire aesthetic in the second half of the Nineties seemingly revolved around the fetishisation of inner-city, disenfranchised black youth: baggy dungarees, boob tubes, oversized anoraks and T-shirts, all featuring his trademark blue, red and white logo, made up a large part of his business. Credible urban artist Aaliyah was hired for Hilfiger's advertising campaign and Naughty by Nature performed at his 1996 show to lend credibility to the brand.

Couture Comeback

Though these carbon-copy designs were a financial success, the less mainstream, credible fashion press largely ignored them in favour of the growing number of conceptual designers whom they cooed over extensively. Comme des Garçons, Miyake, Yamamoto, Margiela and the Antwerp Six were joined by Dutch design duo Viktor & Rolf and a second generation of Japanese and Belgian designers, including Junya Watanabe, Veronique Branquinho, Raf Simons and Olivier Theyskens. In London, British-Turkish Cypriot Hussein Chalayan and fashion's bad boy Alexander McQueen were also making waves. The majority of these designers presented spectacular and often unsettling fashion shows that closely resembled

Above *Hussein Chalayan, Spring/Summer 2000, 'Before Minus Now'. Pink nylon tulle dress laser sculpted from a ball of tulle. It reveals Chalayan's conceptual-led approach to fashion and the body and his interest in the relationship between the body and technology.*

Opposite *Alexander McQueen, Dante, Autumn/Winter 1996. His collections combined exquisite tailoring skills with an idiosyncratic appropriation of history, art and literature. In the age of the glamour vixen, he presented a femininity that was sexual, not conventionally sexy. McQueen's women were intimidating and at times brutal but, like his clothes, they embodied and projected a strength far more complex and interesting than that of most of his contemporaries.*

performance art, which at times overshadowed their innovative ideas and construction techniques and resulted in the more mainstream press ignoring them in favour of easily digestible looks. They nevertheless continued to question the concept of beauty (Comme des Garçons 1997, McQueen 1993–99) and challenge the relationship between fashion and the body (Chalayan 1999, Margiela 1999, Watanabe 1995), and they often attacked the fashion system and its superficial nature (Viktor & Rolf 1996, Margiela 1997). While not as commercially successful as American lifestyle brands, aside from critical acclaim they all managed to carve out a devoted niche customer base.

Mix and Match

Throughout the Nineties, designer fashion thus offered a wide range of choices, from the most basic of items to 'ugly' conceptual clothing. However, while many designers and brands were extremely commercially successful, it must also be remembered that ordinary people, especially the young, often ignored high fashion altogether in favour of their own looks, which they created by mixing different styles and brands with vintage clothes and charity shop finds. This 'mix and match' ethos, which was initially a street style, went mainstream in 1998 with the arrival of HBO's television drama *Sex and the City*. Its fictional protagonist, Carrie Bradshaw, became an immediate fashion icon, and remained so until the series ended in 2004; her glam-designer version of the 'Dress as you please, not as you are told to' style was copied by millions of women. The century that had started with a rigid, dictatorial fashion system, that decreed what women had to wear, thus closed on a note of personal freedom, as women now had a plethora of designers and looks to choose from. Perhaps most importantly, they had the freedom to ignore them all and simply make it up for themselves.

Gianni Versace

Born in Calabria, Italy, Gianni Versace was apprenticed by his seamstress mother at a young age, and after first studying architecture he moved to Milan at the age of 26 to work in fashion. His first solo collection was a success and led to the opening of his own boutique in Milan in 1978.

Throughout the Eighties, his collections received positive reviews and generated steady sales. His extravagant style saw him create stage costumes for pop stars such as Tina Turner and Elton John, while his passion for history led to his designing the costumes for a number of high-profile ballet productions including Richard Strauss's *Josephlegende* (1982), *Lieb und Leid*, based on music by Gustav Mahler (1983), and Maurice Béjart's *Chaka Zulu* (1989). This work was rewarded in 1987 with the prestigious Maschera D'Argento prize.

In 1989 Versace presented his first couture collection, Atelier. It was an exercise in overstatement, glamour and sex: plunging mini dresses were topped with richly embroidered jackets and entire dresses were embellished with crystals and diamantés; this was Alta Moda to excess.

It was in the Nineties that Versace became a household name through a combination of original design, savvy business strategies and celebrity culture. Anna Wintour, editor-in-chief of American *Vogue*, acknowledges that Versace was the first to understand and exploit the value of celebrities by designing their tour wardrobes, attending their parties, putting them in the front row at his shows and, most importantly, by creating the supermodel phenomenon by sending all the top models down the catwalk for his 1991/92 Autumn/Winter collection.

His talent for generating press attention grew his business; by 1993 the diffusion line Versus was added to the Versace stable and became an instant success. Unlike his Atelier range, which was reserved for the ultra-rich, Versus was accessible yet clearly derived from his elite line – the lavish embellishments were merely replaced by bold, eclectic, instantly recognisable prints. The Versace style mixed glamour, sex and classicism and often used innovative materials (aluminium mesh, patent plastics, laser-fused leather and rubber) and bright prints (an eclectic mix of modern art, Technicolor baroque and animal skin). Challenging the limits of good taste, the style came to epitomise Nineties fashion.

Gianni Versace was shot dead in 1997 on the steps of his Miami Beach mansion.

Above *Versace, 1992 charity event in New York with supermodel Claudia Schiffer. The conspicuous gold belt, like all Versace accessories of this period, featured the head of Medusa, the brand's logo.*

Opposite *Versace, Haute Couture, Autumn/ Winter 1995/96, Paris. Versace was known for his experimental fabric use: this dress combines transparent plastic and red metallic Oroton, a metal mesh 'fabric' he devised in the 1980s and used repeatedly in his creations.*

Calvin Klein

The most lucrative of his licences (and the one that would lead to worldwide fame) was for his jeans range: 'Calvins' became the original designer jeans, created simply by putting his name on the back pocket. The craze for designer jeans would increase year on year, reaching its pinnacle in the Eighties; these logo-emblazoned jeans tapped into the spirit of acquisition that dominated at the time, and Klein boosted his sales with shocking advertising.

In 1981 he used the then 15-year-old actress Brooke Shields in a TV commercial. With a seductive look towards the camera she asked: 'You wanna know what comes between me and my Calvins? Nothing.' Klein was accused of inappropriate sexualisation and child pornography, yet sales rocketed.

He used the same shock tactics in the Nineties when he hired Mark Wahlberg in 1992 to advertise his branded underwear. CK underwear had been launched in the early Eighties and, like his jeans, offered nothing new in terms of design but everything in terms of branding. CK courted controversy yet again the following year when they hired the then relatively unknown Kate Moss to pose for CK's Obsession fragrance adverts. The understated black and white image of a naked 17-year-old Moss lying front down on a sofa elicited the same response as the Shields image had, and Moss's youthful thinness (which was in stark contrast to the more curvaceous figures of the supermodels of the time) combined with her vacant stare was now condemned as 'heroin chic' by the media.

Endless column inches were dedicated to the damaging nature of CK adverts (which incidentally continued using Moss, not just for fragrance but also for their jeans and underwear campaigns) and once again the controversy saw the sales and the fame of CK rocket sky high. This ability to sell cheap, uninspiring, mass-produced fashion objects marketed through simple yet provocative advertising as luxury commodities is where the real genius of the company resided, and indeed it is how CK became a dominating Nineties brand.

Calvin Klein studied at the Fashion Institute of Technology in New York and, upon graduating in 1962, worked as a design assistant to Dan Millstein before setting up his own business in 1968. His first collection consisted of simple, elegant dresses and coats, and a substantial order from upmarket New York department store Bonwit Teller soon led to recognition by the fashion world.

Increasing popularity and good sales led to Klein being presented with the Coty award in 1973, and he would go on to win it again for the next three consecutive years. In the Seventies, sportswear, lingerie and a full women's ready-to-wear collection were introduced and a portfolio of licences resulted in scarves, shoes, belts, sunglasses and bedding being produced under the Calvin Klein name.

Opposite *Kate Moss with American model Michael Bergin in 1994 at the Calvin Klein Shop at Macy's Department Store in New York City. Her young age and waifish figure saw her labelled as the 'anti-supermodel' and generated much controversy in the press.*

Left *Less controversial models wearing a sleeveless purple dress and a green cross-strap dress in the Calvin Klein Autumn 1996 fashion show in New York.*

Martin Margiela

Martin Margiela studied fashion at the Royal Academy of Fine Arts in Antwerp, Belgium. He worked as a freelance designer for five years upon graduating in 1979, and moved to Paris in 1985 to work for Jean Paul Gaultier. He founded Maison Margiela in 1989.

His Autumn/Winter 89/90 collection immediately set his house apart. The show had no formal invitations; instead, an ad was taken out in a free Paris paper and the models were dressed in what the press quickly christened 'anti-fashion': tattoo mesh tops, unfinished or cut-up garments. The models themselves were anything but glamorous, which was a stark contrast to what the rest of Paris was presenting. While the more conservative fashionistas grunted, young avant-garde journalists and buyers couldn't get enough and within a few years the brand attained fashion cult status.

Margiela's early collections presented a sort of dysfunctional beauty and included garments made from recycled materials such as broken crockery. Old leather gloves were turned into waistcoats, plastic supermarket bags became vest tops, old army socks were reworked into jumpers. A Fifties ball gown slashed open down the front was worn as a waistcoat, dresses simulated dressmakers' dummies by revealing the normally invisible construction process that underpins couture, and garments were made out of dry-cleaners' plastic. His approach was more than simple recycling, as his use of old clothes 'saved' from flea markets, cut up and remade forced a questioning of history, beauty and luxury.

Like the Japanese designers, Margiela enjoyed playing with proportion and produced oversized garments that drew deliberate attention to the relationship between body and clothes. His work challenged the essence of fashion itself, but far from being gimmicky it was intellectual and showed great consideration and indeed skill. His conceptual approach meant that he soon became referred to as 'the king of deconstruction'.

Margiela himself remained invisible, only giving interviews by fax, never coming out on the catwalk at the end of his shows and refusing to be photographed. He seemingly opposed the designer personality cult and wanted the clothes to speak for themselves. His implicit dislike for the superficial glitz and glamour of the fashion world was also reflected in his shows, which like his fashion were conceptual. They were staged in less than glamorous locations including abandoned hospitals, Metro stations, cemeteries and parts of the city that the majority of the fashion elite never visited, such as poor immigrant areas or seedy red-light districts. Margiela's cult status saw him appointed as creative director at Hermès from 1997 to 2003.

In 2002 the OTB group acquired the brand, allegedly to Margiela's great discontent. After years of rumours and speculation, Maison Margiela released a press statement in 2009 stating: 'Margiela has left the business.'

Opposite *Maison Margiela, ready-to-wear collection, Paris, Autumn 2008. The oversized nature of the garment draws attention to the way fashion has historically manipulated corporeal proportions. It also emphasises the nature of the staple item of the knitted sweater, which we often take for granted.*

Minimalism

The late Eighties saw the development of a new sartorial philosophy that would become a key Nineties fashion player: minimalism. A reaction against Eighties excesses, minimalism was not defined by what it was; rather, by what it lacked. While top designers were loading garments with a plethora of trimmings and creating exaggerated shapes, minimalism presented a look that stripped clothes back to their essence and focused on what they were made of and how they moved.

Minimalism grew out of the popularity of separates, and offered customers wardrobe basics that could be interchanged and built on, as opposed to the total looks presented by brands like Versace, Lacroix and D&G. The term 'basic' can suggest something underwhelming and utilitarian and while minimalism favoured comfort and often took inspiration from workwear and male tailoring, it remained luxurious; it simply presented a more restrained version of luxury that resided in the quality fabrics and the impeccable cut.

Minimal fashions were often described as austere and cold yet their clean, sleek lines and frequently androgynous tailoring ensured their success. The cut made them accessible to a wide variety of shapes and sizes and gave women an alternative to glamorous figure-hugging Italian fashions. Minimalist fashions in part were a wearable interpretation of Eighties Japanese avant-garde fashions in that they translated their gender suspension, colour palette and alternative luxury into digestible format.

Minimalism's popularity meant it quickly found its way into designer collections but the four main propagators of the style were Calvin Klein, Jil Sander, Helmut Lang and Prada. The ad campaigns of all four anchored their style through a shunning of excessive styling and make-up, the use of an often plain white background and a focus on the lived experience of the clothing, not the clothes themselves.

The commercial success of early minimal designers evidenced a desire by women for elegant but comfortable clothing and saw many designers adopt the minimal ethos into their collections. The silhouettes shown here are from Oscar de la Renta's Spring 1997 collection.

⊕ Understated yet chic nature made minimalism appropriate for a variety of occasions and offered a long fashion lifespan. Sander's minimalism was defined by restraint in design paired with a richness of fabric; quality silks, satins, linens and cashmeres cut into relaxed yet perfectly tailored trousers, jackets and shirts.

⊕ Prada employed synthetics such as polyester and nylon with clean precision in their utilitarian minimalism; their simple black or navy nylon backpack became iconic of the decade.

⊕ Lang heavily emphasised structure and forms were often stark in their simplicity. Through the use of cut-outs, asymmetrical cutting and unfinished hems he created a more accessible deconstructionism.

⊕ Klein's interpretation of the style was by far the most digestible and successful, the latter achieved through pricing (significantly lower than the other three) on the one hand and branding/advertising on the other. Klein is the nexus between designer minimalism and its trickled down ready-to-wear application which often crossed over into 'true' basics – such as jeans, plain T-shirts and sleek knitwear.

New Glamour

While minimalism dominated early Nineties catwalks and fashion publications, several journalists voiced their discontent and lamented that the fun had gone out of fashion. The emergence in 1994 of a new glamour look, pejoratively dubbed the 'Power Slut' appears to have been a reaction or an alternative to this simpler, often androgynous style. Headlines such as 'Glamour is in!' and 'dressed to kill' and words such as 'strong', 'sexy' and 'steely' were used to describe this new gloss-lipped, spike-heeled Helmut Newton-esque woman of fashion. Leading brands Versace and Karl Lagerfeld for Chanel but most importantly and successfully Tom Ford, newly appointed at Gucci, all presented their own version. While the first two in many ways simply updated what they had previously presented – stylish power skirt suits – Ford came up with a new ultra-sleek femininity that was sexy but certainly not easy nor to be messed with. His 1995 collection updated Seventies classics such as velvet bellbottom trousers and suits, fitted silk shirts in jewel-like tones worn unbuttoned and bra-less and combined them with car-finish metallic patent boots. In 1996 his evening dresses featured long skirts split up the front and dresses that emphasised hips featuring strategic cut-outs and signature metal belts. Celebrities rushed to get their hands on Gucci by Ford and sales soared. Celebrity endorsement aside, Gucci's adverts were a major factor in the brand's revival; Ford's fashions were presented on self-assured, in-control women who, like Moss in Klein adverts, directly addressed the viewer, but unlike Moss lacked any fragility or ambivalent sexuality. Ford's women were strong, liked sex and were not afraid to show it.

The femme fatale is a stylistic theme that runs through Nineties fashion and that found a variety of different expressions, but its most extreme incarnation was arguably the one created by fashion's bad boy Alexander McQueen. Whereas Ford's women were assertive, McQueen's were positively terrifying.

_____ Madonna attended the 1995 MTV Video Music awards in teal silk blouse paired with hip-hugging silk trousers. When asked what she was wearing, she gushed: 'Gucci, Gucci, Gucci.' Tom Ford identified this moment of celebrity endorsement as key to his success.

● The Nineties saw an exploration of femininity and a fascination with new possibilities; it seems fashion was sartorially representing the third-wave feminist debates that emerged at the start of the decade and that tried foregrounded freedom from gender expectations, a liberation from societal norms and sexual liberation. The androgynous models in Sander's adverts, Ford's 'power sluts' and McQueen's savage goddesses in this context all represent options in and limitation to those debates.

● McQueen's shows managed to shock even the most cutting-edge journalists. His women were dressed in low-riding bumsters, see-through net dresses worn over militaristic leather underwear, dresses made of clingfilm, a bodice of moulded plastic encasing worms or PVC trousers cut so low pubic hair was showing, and styled as near demonic uber-women.

Burberry Check

The final years of the Nineties were marked by a rather uncommon key look phenomenon: a look that was not a look at all but rather a print – the Burberry Nova print. Burberry, which in the late Nineties became *the* fashion label, was founded in 1856. It was a company that specialised in outdoor wear not fashion, the go-to company in the late nineteenth and early twentieth centuries for gabardine jackets, riding wear, trench coats (created by Burberry for the British Army in World War One) and, later, aviation wear. The famous check was developed in the Twenties as a coat lining fabric. The brand remained popular for its staples throughout the post-war years but by the Nineties its identity had become outdated and Burberry products were mostly associated with old people and tourists.

In 1997 to resurrect the brand Rose Marie Bravo (who as president of Saks Fifth Avenue had turned the sleepy retailer into a fashion-forward award-winning business) was hired as chief executive officer. She immediately spotted the brand's heritage potential but realised that to succeed it had to appeal to a younger audience. To achieve this she hired Italian-American designer Roberto Menichetti to design a range that capitalised on the brand's history while dropping that target customer's age by thirty years. His answer came in the form of a rejuvenated collection that played around with the house's Nova check, which he applied to trench coats, dresses, shirts, skirts, bags and even bikinis. To attract a young, aspirational clientele he extended the range to also include a host of cheaper yet carefully branded check items including scarves, umbrellas, belts and key rings. Kate Moss was enlisted as the new face of Burberry and her working-class roots combined with her high fashion credentials presented the brand as the perfect mix of luxury, authenticity and edginess. Sales figures quickly rocketed, celebrities and fashionistas embraced the 'new' Burberry and the check quickly became the must-have look.

By the end of the decade the Nova check was omnipresent and fast becoming associated with those the press labelled as 'undesirable', by which they mostly meant working-class non-elitist consumers. Burberry was becoming the victim of its own success, but also a clear case study of what would face the industry in the decade to come: the precarious and constant balancing act of accessibility and exclusivity.

● The success of the Burberry check led to endless high-street interpretations and, more problematically, illegal (and mostly inferior) copies. As *The Times* newspaper aptly observed: 'The clever but naïve idea to print a few affordable Burberry headscarves and bikinis to rid itself of its stuffy image turned into a highly contagious virus.'

Selected bibliography

Adorned in Dreams: Fashion and Modernity
E. Wilson (2003) I. B. Tauris

Against Fashion: Clothing as Art, 1850–1930 R. Stern,
E. W. Godwin, O. Wilde, J. F. M. Hoffmann, H. van de
Velde, G. Balla, & S. Delaunay (2004) MIT Press

Balenciaga L. E. Miller (2007) V&A Publications

The Berg Companion to Fashion V. Steele (2010) Berg

Christian Dior: The Early Years 1947–1957 E. De Rethy
and J. L. Perreau (2001) Thames & Hudson

Coco Chanel: The Legend and the Life J. Picardie (2013)
HarperCollins

*Couture & Commerce: The Transatlantic Fashion Trade
in the 1950s* A. Palmer (2001) UBC Press

Couture Culture: A Study in Modern Art and Fashion
N. J. Troy (2003) MIT Press

Couture, The Great Designers C. R. Milbank (1985)
Stewart Tabori & Chang

The Cutting Edge A. De La Haye (1998) V&A
Publications

The Empire of Fashion: Dressing Modern Democracy
G. Lipovetsky & R. Sennett, (1994) Princeton
University Press

Fashion C. Breward (2003) Oxford University Press

Fashion: The Century of the Designer 1900–1999
C. Seeling (ed.) (2000) Konemann

*Fashion at the Edge: Spectacle, Modernity and
Deathliness* C. Evans (2003) Yale University Press

Fashion & Fashion Designers G. O'Hara Callan &
C. Glover (2008) Thames & Hudson

Fashion Italian Style V. Steele (2003) Yale
University Press

Fashion: The Key Concepts J. Craik (2009) Berg

Fashion Sourcebook 1920s E. Dirix & C. Fiell (2011) Fiell

Fashion Sourcebook 1930s E. Dirix & C. Fiell (2011) Fiell

Fashion Sourcebook 1940s E. Dirix (2013) Goodman
Books

Fashion Sourcebook 1970s E. Dirix (2014) Carlton Books

King of Fashion: The Autobiography of Paul Poiret
P. Poiret (1931) J. B. Lippincott

Madeleine Vionnet: Puriste de la Mode (2009)
Les Arts Decoratifs

Nothing in Itself: Complexions of Fashion (vol. 24)
H. Blau (1999) Indiana University Press

Old Clothes, New Looks: Second-hand Fashion (no. 35)
A. Palmer (2005) Berg

Christian Lacroix on Fashion Christian Lacroix and
Patrick Mauriès (2007) Thames & Hudson

Paris Fashion. A Cultural History V. Steele (1988)
Oxford University Press

Swinging Sixties C. Breward, D. Gilbert and J. Lister
(2006) V&A Publications

Shocking!: The Art and Fashion of Elsa Schiaparelli
D. Blum (2003) Yale University Press

*Through the Looking Glass: A History of Dress from 1860
to the Present Day* E. Wilson (1989) BBC Publications

Twentieth Century Fashion in Detail C. Wilcox and
V. Mendes (2009) V&A Publications

Women & Fashion: A New Look C. Evans and
M. Thornton (1989) Quartet

Women of Fashion: Twentieth-century Designers
V. Steele (1991) Rizzoli

Yves St Laurent F. Chenoune (2010) Abrams

WEBSITES

www.lesartsdecoratifs.fr

www.metmuseum.org/works_of_art/
the_costume_institute

www.modeaparis.com

www.style.com

www.thamesandhudson.com

www.vam.co.uk

Image credits

Xabier Armendaritz/CC-BY-2.0 128

Jan Arkesteijn/CC-BY-SA 3.0 nl 139

Brooklyn Museum Online Collection 22

© **Corbis** 62, 211

Corinne Coulomb and Francine Thiercelin on behalf of the family of Jeanne Margaine-Lacroix 28

German Federal Archive 100

Getty Images: 10 Popperfoto, 19 Ullstein Bild, 24 Keystone-France, 31 General Photographic Agency, 32 and 34 Popperfoto, 36 Felix, 39 (left) Heritage Images, 44 APIC, 47 Ullstein Bild, 48 Print Collector, 49 Keystone-France, 50 APIC, 51 Popperfoto, 54 Branger, 59 (bottom) Photo 12/UIG, 60 Sasha, 64 Ullstein Bild, 67 Luigi Diaz, 69 Chicago History Museum, 71 Roger Viollet, 72 Lipnitzki, 74 Brooke, 76 Chicago History Museum, 79 Graphicaartis, 81 DEA/A. Dagli Orti, 82 Print Collector, 84 Archive Photos, 86 APIC, 87 and 89 Lipnitzki, 88 Chicago History Museum, 90 John Kobal Foundation, 91 and 92 George Hurrell, 96 Eugene Robert Richee, 99 Underwood Archives, 101 Keystone-France, 102 Frank Scherschel, 104 Chicago History Museum, 105 Print Collector, 107 Bertrand Rindoff Petroff, 108 Chicago History Museum, 109 Eliot Elisofon, 111 Pat English, 112 IWM/Getty Images, 114, 116 and 119 Keystone-France, 120 Terry Fincher, 121 Kammerman, 123 Gjon Mili, 125 Chicago History Museum, 126 Nat Farbman, 127 Ullstein Bild, 129 Chicago History Museum, 131 RDA, 132 Kurt Hutton, 134 Archive Photos, 136 Nat Farbman, 140 Keystone-France, 141 Bill Ray, 143 and 145 Keystone-France, 147 Ullstein Bild, 148 David Lees, 149 Rolls Press/Popperfoto, 150 Oli Scarff, 151 Keystone, 152 Justin de Villeneuve, 154 Popperfoto, 156 Reg Lancaster, 159 The LIFE Picture Collection, 161 Justin de Villeneuve, 165 Waring Abbott, 167 The LIFE Images Collection, 168 Jack Robinson, 169 Susan Wood/Getty Images, 171 Keystone-France, 172 Ron Bull, 174 Keystone, 176 Justin de Villeneuve, 179 AFP, 180 Erin Combs, 182, 185 and 186 Gamma-Rapho, 187 Erin Combs, 188 Foc Kan, 189 Gamma-Rapho, 191 Bernard Weil, 192 AFP, 194 Ullstein Bild, 196 Barbara Alper, 199 Marion Curtis, 201 Keith Beaty, 202 Bertrand Rindoff Petroff, 204, 205, 207 and 209 AFP, 206 Ron Galella, Ltd, 208 Jim Smeal, 212 Evan Agostini, 214 The LIFE Picture Collection, 216 Ron Galella, Ltd

HellN/CC-2.0 181

Lynsey Erin Hirth 106 (top)

LACMA 21 (top)

Library of Congress 26, 30, 39 (right), 43 (top), 61, 63, 65, 68, /Toni Frissell 122, /Carl Van Vechten 130

Erik Liljeroth, Nordiska Museet/ CC-BY-4.0 124

Mabalu/CC-BY-SA-2.0 162, /CC-BY-SA-2.0 190

Maurilbert/CC-BY-3.0 170

MCAD Library/CC-BY-2.0 70

National Archives (UK) 139 (top)

supplied courtesy of **Susie Ralph** 28, 29

Shutterstock.com: 6/Everett Collection, 11 (bottom) /Grzegorz Petrykowski, 13 /cdrin, 45 / LiliGraphie, 94 /Everett Collection, 183 /360b, 200 /Featureflash

Index

Acknowledgements

The author wishes to express her gratitude to
fellow-author Susie Ralph for her help in sourcing
images of Jeanne Margaine-Lacroix.